BACK TO
THE BEYOND

BOB & KATIE,
THANK YOU FOR ALL OF
YOUR SUPPORT!

BACK TO THE BEYOND

EXPLORING NEAR-DEATH EXPERIENCES THROUGH HYPNOSIS

Adam S. Dince, MBA, Certified Hypnotherapist

ISBN 13: 978-1-63489-487-6

Library of Congress Catalog Number has been applied for.
Printed in the United States of America
First Printing: 2022

26 25 24 23 22   5 4 3 2 1

Cover design by Emily Mahon
Interior design by Maggie Villaume

Wise Ink Creative Publishing
807 Broadway St NE
Suite 46
Minneapolis, MN 55413

I would like to dedicate this book to the following:

My dad, Bert Dince: Thank you for being such a wonderful father, teacher, and friend in both life and the afterlife.

Cari Moisan: Thank you for being my wonderful hypnotherapy instructor, mentor, and dear friend. This research and book wouldn't exist without you.

My guru, Ram Dass: Thank you for being my spiritual guide on this beautiful journey through life.

Dr. Eben Alexander: Your book Proof of Heaven *was instrumental to me finding peace with the physical death. Your book* Seeking Heaven *taught me to how meditate and connect with All That Is.*

Dr. Michael Newton: Your books introduced me to the concepts of using hypnosis to regress people back to past life and between lives memories. Your books led me to experiencing my own past life regression, which forever changed my perception of what it means to be an eternal soul. Without you, I would not have found my passion for hypnotherapy.

Finally, so much love and gratitude for all of the beautiful souls who left their bodies, returned, and shared their stories with the world. And extra special thanks to each of the participants who volunteered for the research in this book.

"These bodies we live in, and the ego that identifies with it [sic], are just like the old family car. They are functional entities in which our Soul travels through our incarnation. But when they are used up, they die. The most graceful thing to do is to just allow them to die peacefully and naturally—to 'let go lightly.' Through it all, who we are is Soul . . . and when the body and the ego are gone, the Soul will live on, because the Soul is eternal. Eventually, in some incarnation, when we've finished our work, our Soul can merge back into the One . . . back into God . . . back into the Infinite. In the meantime, our Soul is using bodies, egos, and personalities to work through the karma of each incarnation."

– Ram Dass

"Try and imagine what it will be like to go to sleep and never wake up. Think about that.

Children think about it.

It's one of the great wonders of life.

What will it be like to go to sleep and never wake up?

And if you think long enough about that, something will happen to you. You will find out, among other things, that it will pose the next question to you. What was it like to wake up after having never gone to sleep?"

– Alan Watts, "The Real You"

CONTENTS

INTRODUCTION

What happens to us when our physical bodies die? Do we have souls that continue on? Is there an afterlife? Is there a heaven? Is there a hell? Do we reunite with our loved ones who have crossed over? I began grappling with these questions in 2005 after losing my dad in a tragic car accident.

Shortly after my dad crossed over, a dear friend recommended that I speak with an intuitive that she'd consulted with for years. She swore that this guy was the best in the business. Prior to my dad's passing, I never would have considered speaking to a medium. I labeled them scam artists who take advantage of those suffering from grief and loss. But my heart was so broken and empty that I was willing to try anything. So, I moved forward and booked a session with the medium. My conversation with the medium was a life-changing experience. He knew things that only my dad and I were privy to. And frankly, the medium knew things that I didn't know about my dad prior to our session. Information that I validated after our appointment by asking family and friends. The mediumship session opened up my consciousness to the idea that there's far more to our existence than meets the eye.

Throughout my years of research and various pursuits of understanding what happens to us after we die, I kept coming across stories/accounts of near-death experiences (NDEs). Essentially, NDEs occur when a person's physical body briefly dies, grows severely ill, or experiences significant trauma, and the soul/essence/spirit leaves the body. When the person is eventually brought back to life or wakes up, the soul pops back into the physical, and she or he remembers what was experienced while out-of-body.

While many of the NDE accounts were brilliant and undeniably believed by the experiencer, I remained cautiously skeptical about whether or not these accounts were legitimate. I kept coming back to the question, "What if an NDE is nothing more than a vivid dream the brain has while a person is nearing death?" Dreams can seem believably real. Surely you've had a dream where you questioned whether it was real or not.

Then, I came across the book *Proof of Heaven* by Dr. Eben Alexander, MD. Eben Alexander's NDE account is often cited in papers and books as proof that NDEs are real, and it's difficult to dispute his accounts. Dr. Alexander, a well-respected neurosurgeon, was brought into a medically induced coma for seven days after contracting bacterial meningoencephalitis. During his weeklong coma, Dr. Alexander experienced one of the most profound NDE accounts I've read to date. In my opinion, what sets Dr. Alexander's book apart from others is how he brilliantly weaves his mystical experiences while out-of-body together with his adamant position that science can't explain how his brain (given the bacterial meningoencephalitis) could have been able to recall what he experienced while out-of-body.

> *"If one had asked me before my coma how much a patient would remember after such severe meningitis, I would have answered 'nothing' and been thinking in the back of my mind that no one would recover from such an illness, at least not to the point of being able to discuss their memories. Thus, you can imagine my surprise at remembering an elaborate and rich odyssey from deep within coma that comprised more than 20,000 words by the time I had written it all down during the six weeks following my return from the hospital. My older son, Eben Alexander IV, who was majoring in neuroscience at the University of Delaware at the time, advised me to record everything I could remember before I read anything about near-death experiences (NDEs), physics or cosmology. I dutifully did so, in spite of an intense yearning to read everything I could about those subjects, based on the stunning character of my coma experience.*
>
> *My meningoencephalitis had been so severe that my original memories from within coma did not include any recollections whatsoever from my life before coma, including language and any knowledge of humans or this universe. That 'scorched earth' intensity was the setting for a profound spiritual experience that took me beyond space and time to what seemed like the origin of all existence."*

> – *Dr. Eben Alexander*

Dr. Alexander's book made me a believer in near-death experiences and the eternal nature of our essence. With *Proof of Heaven*, all of my previous NDE research had become that much more meaningful. I was a believer.

While studying NDEs, I discovered that many who have had near-death experiences believe in reincarnation. That our souls live many physical lives in either human or nonhuman form. And, while it felt safe for me to believe in life after death, believing in past lives/reincarnation was not a concept I was comfortable with. I didn't want to consider an option where our souls come back into the physical and do this dance all over again. Life is hard. Why would we want or choose to live in a body more than once?

However, after years of research around reincarnation, I couldn't deny the validity of the accounts I read and people I interviewed. One of the strongest proofs of reincarnation that I found was the brilliant account of a three-year-old boy who remembered his past life, was able to locate his dead body, and then identified the man who killed him (Global Heart, 2017). I became obsessed with researching past lives. And the obsession with past lives grew even more intense after reading Dr. Michael Newton's book *Journey of Souls*. In *Journey of Souls*, Dr. Newton provides transcripts of some of his clients' past life regression sessions. The accounts are brilliant! Dr. Newton's book made me a believer.

Journey of Souls also opened my eyes to the possibility of exploring a past life regression myself, which became the next part of my journey. Shortly after finishing Newton's book, I met Eric Christopher. Eric, who studied with Dr. Newton, is a brilliant hypnotherapist highly skilled in past life and life between lives regression. Life between lives (LBL) regression is a modality of hypnotherapy pioneered by Dr. Newton and practiced by many hypnotherapists trained to do so. My first meeting with Eric was for an intake session where he guided me through what hypnotherapy is, how regression works, and what to expect when we met for our next session, the past life regression. He also dug deep into my personal journey; we spoke about my fascination with past lives and near-death experiences, and all things related to the mystical side of spirituality. I immediately clicked with Eric.

Two weeks later, Eric and I met for my past life regression session. Prior to beginning the regression process, Eric asked me if I had any questions. I said, "Yes, as a matter of fact, I do. How many of your clients think this whole regression thing is a bunch of hooey and won't work?" Eric replied, "Most of my new clients have doubts about their ability to be hypnotized and experience a regression. But I assure you that you'll be just fine." And with that, my mind and heart were at ease, and I was ready for the regression experience.

It's really difficult to put my past life regression experience into words. How can one possibly describe something so mystical and profound with the limitations of human-created language? What I can say is, to actually see a past life with your own mind's eye is life changing. In a matter of two and a half hours, I went from someone who *believed* in the concepts of past lives and reincarnation to someone who *knew* that we live many lives.

And as I sat in my car, waiting for it to warm up after leaving Eric's office, I knew that part of my purpose in life was to become a hypnotherapist and support others on their journeys to find peace with life, death, and who they are as a soul. And to be fulfilling this purpose now is one of the greatest honors and pleasures of my life.

I am certified as a hypnotherapist through the Institute of Neuro-Linguistic Programming (INLP) Center and as a hypnotist through the International Hypnosis Federation (IHF). I'm also a Reiki Master Teacher, which allows me to integrate energy healing as needed within regression sessions. All of my hypnotherapy sessions are facilitated virtually, allowing me to work with past life, between lives, and current life regression clients across the globe. In fact, as you'll read in this book, two of the seven volunteers who volunteered for this near-death experience research are based outside of the United States.

Now, allow me to connect the dots between hypnotic regression and near-death experiences as it pertains to the research in this book. As I studied people's accounts of NDEs, one thing I learned is that not everyone's recollection of their NDE is as vivid as Dr. Alexander's. For many, NDE memories fade as time goes on. This insight led me to ponder whether or not I could hypnotically regress people who had NDEs back to their out-of-body experience (OBE). And if I was able to regress people back to their near-death/out-of-body experience, would they be able to remember what they'd forgotten over time? And, could they find closure to their experience?

And from there, my hypothesis was born. Since hypnotic regression allows subjects to revisit memories of experiences they've had in this life or in past lives, I *would* be able to regress people back to their memories of their near-death experience.

And as you'll read in the upcoming chapters, what happened was much more profound than regressing participants back to their NDE memories. What many experienced was a journey to the dimensions/planes where the source of mystical experiences originates; a journey back to the beyond.

RESEARCH
METHODOLOGY

B elow is a summary of how the research for this book was
conducted.

- Seven people who experienced NDEs volunteered to be put
under hypnosis to explore the memories of their near-death
experience(s).

- Once a participant agreed to be part of the research,
I scheduled an hour-long virtual intake session facilitated
through Zoom. The intake process is important. In order for
someone to successfully enter a state of hypnosis, they have
to trust and feel comfortable with their hypnotherapist.
So, part of this intake process involved developing good
rapport with participants.

- Also, during intake, I made it a point to provide a thorough
description about how hypnotic regression works, my
regression protocol, and what to expect during the
regression session.

- Then, participants shared their NDE stories, which were
recorded and later transcribed for use in this book.

After participants shared their NDE account, they provided me with a list of questions and areas of closure they wished to address while in hypnosis. Finally, a date and time was set for the NDE regression session.

Regression sessions followed the format below.

- To ensure participants understood what to expect in the regression, I again reviewed the regression protocol that we discussed during our intake session and answered any remaining questions.

- Once all questions were addressed, I asked participants to get into a comfortable position and close their eyes. I also asked that they keep their phone or microphone nearby so that I could clearly hear their voice.

- Next, I induced participants into a deep state of hypnosis. Once in hypnosis, I asked participants to visualize a hallway with many doors, with each of the doors representing a relevant experience to explore. Then, I had participants find a door that appeared to stand out from the rest, with that door representing the portal they would walk through. Once participants identified the door, I suggested that they walk to the door, but not walk through it yet.

- Then, once standing in front of the door, I connected participants with some of the NDE-related emotions, feelings, and beliefs they shared during their intake.

- Once connected to the aforementioned emotions, feelings, and beliefs, I had them walk through the door.

- And once participants walked through the door, they regressed to a memory or place where they were able to connect back with their NDE in their own unique way.

- During the session, we revisited as much of participants' NDEs as they were allowed to see. This provided the volunteers the opportunity to receive whatever closure they

were seeking and to ask any other questions about their
current life.

- Finally, once the NDE was fully explored, I brought
  participants out of hypnosis and we discussed
  the experience.

All of the NDE regression sessions were complimentary. And in
return for the complimentary session, participants agreed to let
me publish the transcripts of the regression sessions in this book.

As you read this book, you'll see that each person's account is
broken into three sections:

1. The subject's story/memory of their near-death experience
2. Questions or areas of closure that the subject asked to
   explore during the NDE regression
3. The transcript of the NDE regression

For those new to the topic of near-death experiences, out-of-body
experiences, and/or hypnotic regression, the next three chapters of
this book offer brief overviews.

- Chapter I introduces the topic of out-of-body experiences
  (OBEs). Everyone who has a memorable NDE essentially has
  an out-of-body experience. So, it's important to understand
  what OBEs are and how they work.
- Chapter II provides a light background into what NDEs are
  and why I believe that they are real.
- Chapter III introduces you to hypnosis and regression, which
  are the techniques I used to guide NDE subjects back to the
  memories of their experiences.

CHAPTER I

OUT-OF-BODY EXPERIENCES (OBEs)

Before we go into detail about near-death experiences, it's important to touch on the topic of out-of-body experiences, since most NDEs involve out-of-body phenomena.

An out-of-body experience, in its simplest definition, occurs when people perceive the world around them from a location outside of their physical body. I first learned about out-of-body experiences in the 2010 film *Insidious*. *Insidious* is the fictional story of a boy who is able to leave his physical body, and his "astral" body travels to a space called "the Further." In the Further, the boy meets evil spirits who attempt to keep him from returning home, while other spirits attempt to enter into the boy's physical body that had been left vacant.

Years later, I came across a modern-day mystic, Ryan Cropper, who is quite skilled at what's referred to as "astral projection." Astral projection is when a person's astral body leaves the physical body and travels the earth plane or other dimensions. The astral body is one of the seven layers of our aura. It's the layer of the aura connected to our heart chakra and is our energetic footprint that allows us to have out-of-body experiences.

Ryan's videos describing his travels were brilliantly fascinating. I couldn't believe that out-of-body experiences were achievable. In addition to sharing stories of his astral projection expeditions, Ryan also offers online classes that teach people how to astral project. If you explore Ryan's YouTube channel or belong to his Facebook group, you'll find that many of his students have learned how to successfully leave their body. I did meet with Ryan for an hour-long session, where he shared his "how to leave your body" secrets with me, but I just didn't have the time or a quiet space to practice and learn.

While there are people who are born with the ability to astral project and people who take the time to learn the skill, most people who have out-of-body experiences find that they happen spontaneously and not very often. I experienced my OBE in the summer of 2019 and it hasn't happened again since. I recall lying in bed trying to fall asleep. Our neighbors were having a party in their backyard that went well into the night. And as I lay in bed with my eyes closed, trying to relax enough to fall asleep, my body began to tingle. I recalled reading in a variety of books on the topic of astral travel that when a person is close to "popping out" of their body, they may experience sleep paralysis. People often describe their experiences with sleep paralysis as frightening. Sleep paralysis purportedly involves experiencing a very intense buzzing or vibration throughout the entirety of the body, accompanied by the inability to move the extremities. One person told me that sleep paralysis felt like something was sitting on his chest holding him down, like a demon.

I didn't feel any of the intense/scary aforementioned sensations. The vibrations I felt in my body were peaceful, if anything. Just a slight tingle. And I began to wonder if this was my chance to experience an OBE. So, I did what Ryan Cropper told me to do once I achieved sleep paralysis—I tried to quickly sit up in bed, which caused my astral body to pop out. And there I was, floating freely above my body staring down at myself in bed with my back facing the ceiling. The first thought that came into my mind was, "OK, now how do I move around?" I wanted to travel elsewhere. Even to simply visit another room in the house. But, before I had the chance to try, the neighbors cranked the music up and I popped right back into my body.

While I was disappointed that my out-of-body experience only lasted a few moments, I was absolutely thrilled that I had experienced an OBE. It was proof to me that we are so much more than our physical selves.

In addition to astral projection and astral traveling, out-of-body experiences are also common for people who use plant medicines, dimethyltryptamine (DMT), and synthetic drugs like LSD. One of my favorite books on the topic of psychedelic-induced out-of-body experiences is *DMT: The Spirit Molecule: A Doctor's Revolutionary Research into the Biology of Near-Death and Mystical Experiences* by Dr. Rick Strassman. In this book, Dr. Strassman details the findings of his government-funded human research about DMT's effects through clinical trials.

"The most interesting results were that high doses of DMT seemed to allow the consciousness of our volunteers to enter an out-of-body, freestanding, independent realm of existence, inhabited by beings of light who oftentimes were expecting the volunteers and with whom the volunteers interacted."

– Dr. Rick Strassman

CHAPTER II

NEAR-DEATH EXPERIENCES (NDEs)

N ow that we've touched on out-of-body experiences, let's cover near-death experiences. Essentially, in a near-death experience, people who are close to death, ill, traumatized, or who briefly die leave their physical bodies. Some souls stay close to their bodies (e.g., in their hospital room), and others travel to the "beyond." Some have no memory of anything happening at all. Simply like falling asleep and waking up without a dream to recall.

Local and Nonlocal NDEs

I categorize memorable or vivid NDEs in one of two categories: local and nonlocal.

Local NDE: In a local NDE, the soul leaves the body but stays in the physical earth plane. For example:

Singer-songwriter Pam Reynolds experienced a massive aneurysm in her brain stem. In order for the surgeons to operate, they had to put Pam into a nearly comatose state.

When the operation began, the surgeons taped shut Reynolds's eyes and put molded speakers in her ears. The ear speakers, which made clicking sounds as loud as a jet plane taking off, allowed the surgeons to measure her brain stem activity and let them know when they could drain her blood.

"I was lying there on the gurney minding my own business, seriously unconscious, when I started to hear a noise," Reynolds recalled. "It was a natural D, and as the sound continued—I don't know how to explain this, other than to go ahead and say it—I popped up out of the top of my head." She said she found herself looking down at the operating table. She could see twenty people around the table and hear what sounded like a dentist's drill. She looked at the instrument in the surgeon's hand.

"It was an odd-looking thing," she said. "It looked like the handle on my electric toothbrush." Reynolds observed the Midas Rex bone mill the surgeons used to cut open her head, the drill bits, and the case, which looked like the one where her father kept his socket wrenches. Then she noticed a surgeon at her left groin.

"I heard a female voice say, 'Her arteries are too small.' And Dr. Spetzler—I think it was him—said, 'Use the other side,'" Reynolds recalled.

Soon after, the surgeons began to lower her body temperature to 60 degrees. It was about that time that Reynolds believes she noticed a tunnel and bright light. She eventually flatlined completely, and the surgeons drained the blood out of her head.

During her near-death experience, she said she chatted with her dead grandmother and uncle, who escorted her back to the operating room. She said as they looked down on her body, she could hear the Eagles song "Hotel California" playing in the operating room as the doctors restarted her heart. She said her body looked like a train wreck, and she said she didn't want to return.

"My uncle pushed me," she said, laughing. "And when I hit the body, the line in the song was, 'You can check out anytime you like, but you can never leave.' And I opened my eyes and I said, 'You know, that is really insensitive!'" Afterwards, Reynolds assumed she had been hallucinating. But a year later, she mentioned the details to her neurosurgeon. Spetzler said her account matched his memory.

"From a scientific perspective," he said, "I have absolutely no explanation about how it could have happened." (Hagerty, 2009)

Nonlocal NDE: In a nonlocal NDE, the soul/astral body leaves the physical body and travels to another realm/dimension. Within my research, most people who experience a nonlocal NDE refer to the place they visit as "home." And in their visit home, they may meet a whole cast of beings, such as their spirit guides, soul families, deceased family members, God, etc. When they enter back into their bodies, they have extremely vivid memories of the experience.

In her book, *The Five Lessons of Life*, my dear friend Carrie Kohan details her two NDEs. That's right, Carrie died twice and had two completely different near-death experiences. In her first NDE, Carrie's soul traveled to a place that she refers to as hell. In her second, she travels to a place she calls heaven. During her second NDE, Carrie was shown much about her life, her purpose in life, and a message to bring back and share with the world. She even experienced watching herself plan out her current life before incarnating as Carrie. I conducted an hour-long interview with Carrie on my podcast, *The SpiritWoke Podcast*, where she shares her story and lessons learned. You can find it at https://www.spiritwoke.com/five-lessons-of-life/.

And, of course, you'll find NDE accounts of this book's research participants as you get into further chapters.

How Do We Know That NDEs Are Real?

While Dr. Eben Alexander's account in his book *Proof of Heaven* is undeniably real, here are a few other reasons to believe.

Dr. Kenneth Ring conducted a study where he investigated fourteen people who were blind from birth that had NDEs. Nine out of the fourteen people examined in the study reported vision during their experiences.

"Our findings revealed that blind persons, including those blind from birth, do report classic NDEs of the kind common to sighted persons; that the great preponderance of blind persons claim to see during NDEs and OBEs; and that occasionally claims of visually based knowledge that could not have been obtained by normal means can be independently corroborated. We present and evaluate various explanations of these findings before arriving at an interpretation based on the concept of transcendental awareness." (Ring & Cooper, 1997)

Additionally, there is a very specific type of near-death experience that is classified as a veridical NDE. The University of Virginia defines a veridical NDE as when, ". . . experiencers acquire verifiable information that they could not have obtained by any normal means. For example, some experiencers report seeing events going on at some distant location, such as another room of the hospital; or an experiencer might meet a deceased loved one who then communicates verifiable information the experiencer had not known." (Near-Death Experiences (NDEs))

Veridical NDEs are not a new phenomenon. In fact, accounts of veridical NDEs go back to the year 1882, in which the person who experienced the NDE, upon return to his body, reported his perceptions while out of body. His accounts were later verified to be accurate. (Holden & James, 2009)

A brilliant example of a veridical NDE is documented in a report published in 2013 in the *Journal of Near-Death Studies* titled "A Near-Death Experience with Veridical Perception Described by a Famous Heart Surgeon and Confirmed by His Assistant Surgeon." In this research, Dr. Lloyd Rudy shares an account of a man he was treating for an aneurysm. After the surgery to treat the aneurysm was complete, it appeared as if his patient wouldn't be able to recover, and attempts to save his life were ended. Shortly after turning off the machines that were keeping the patient alive, the patient's heartbeat returned. And shortly thereafter, the patient's blood pressure normalized and was revived without any damage to his brain.

After a few days of recovery, the patient shared with Dr. Rudy and his medical team what he experienced while out of body.

"I saw you and Dr. Cattaneo standing in the doorway with your arms folded, talking. I saw the—I didn't know where the anesthesiologist was, but he came running back in. And I saw all of these Post-its [Post-it® notes] sitting on this TV screen. And what those were, were any call I got, the nurse would write down who called and the phone number and stick it on the monitor, and then the next Post-it would stick to that Post-it, and then I'd have a string of Post-its of phone calls I had to make. He described that.

I mean, there is no way he could have described that before the operation, because I didn't have any calls, right?

"He was up there. He described the scene, things that there is no way he knew. I mean, he didn't wake up in the operating room and see all this. I mean he was out and was out for, I don't know, even a day or two while we recovered him in the intensive care unit. So what does that tell you? Was that his soul up there?" (Rivas & Dirven, 2010)

Years later, Dr. Rudy's assistant surgeon, Dr. Cattaneo validated the patient's account. Cattaneo added that normally during a surgery, the patient's eyes are closed—taped closed. In other words, there's no way the patient would have been able to see the Post-it notes. There's no scientific explanation for how the patient observed what he did.

Please note that in the patient's account, he also noted seeing a bright white light at the end of a tunnel. (Smit, 2008)

Rounding Out the Topic of NDEs

Often times, people who experience NDEs return to their bodies with powerful psychic-related gifts and abilities. Also, many NDEers return with a better understanding of their purpose in this incarnation. However, while many people do return from their out-of-body experiences with brilliant tales, abilities, and the feeling of a renewed zest for life, that's not the story for everyone.

For some who return from an NDE, a perpetual dark night of the soul never seems to end. Think of the dark night of the soul as a sort of spiritual depression. Imagine that your physical body is dead, you leave your body and then go on to experience what it's like to be "home," in other words, in the afterlife. While you're home on the other side, you're greeted by family members and friends who have crossed over. You reunite with pets whom you loved. You meet your angels, spirit guides, and even God. You're in the place of pure love. There's no more worry and all fear is gone. You're essentially experiencing nirvana. And then, Boom! You've woken back up in your physical body wanting nothing more than to return to the place your soul just visited.

Imagine just how tough it must be to come back to our human existence. An existence where we have bills to pay, perceived problems, and, of course, the physical injuries sustained from the experience that caused the NDE.

Also, not everyone remembers all of the details of their NDE when they return to their bodies. And even those who once had a crystal-clear recollection of what happened during their NDE find that the memories fade over the years. In fact, many of the NDEers I've interviewed and spoken with expressed the desire to fill gaps in their memory. Additionally, many NDEers have questions they would like to have asked while on the other side. Questions that, if answered, would provide closure to many of the situations they have experienced in their current incarnation. You may be thinking to yourself, why wouldn't NDEers ask these questions when they had the chance to? Imagine meeting God in an out-of-body experience. The overwhelming nature of that experience might be so powerful that you don't think to ask questions pertinent to your life. Questions like, "What's my purpose in life?" or "Why do I have so much pain?" This is where my vision for the research behind *Back to the Beyond* comes into play. I pondered, could I use hypnotherapy to take people back to their NDEs to get the answers and the closure they seek? The answer is a resounding yes! And, as you'll read in the book, most had more profound experiences than simply regressing back to the memories of what happened after they left their bodies.

CHAPTER III

HYPNOTIC REGRESSION & NEAR-DEATH EXPERIENCES

OVERVIEW

During hypnotherapy intake sessions with new clients, one of the first questions I ask is, "What do you know about hypnosis?" Most of the answers are similar to, "I once saw a hypnotist at a fair who put a bunch of people under hypnosis and made them bark like dogs. You're not going to make me bark like a dog, are you?" This state fair–like show utilizes hypnotic suggestion, which involves putting subjects' minds into a deeply relaxed state. And in this deeply relaxed hypnotic state, the subconscious mind opens to suggestion. When the hypnotist says, "When I count to three and snap my fingers, you will bark like a dog," what the hypnotist is doing is making a hypnotic suggestion to the subject. The word "suggestion" is the perfect word to describe what's happening. The hypnotist is not forcing the subject to bark like a dog; the performer is simply suggesting that the subject take the action. If the subject was asked to do something that he or she wouldn't be open to doing outside of the hypnotic state, the participant would immediately come out of hypnosis. In other words, the noise of the inner conflict would pull the subject out of the hypnotic state. Keep in mind that someone in a hypnotic trance does not disassociate from the conscious mind. The conscious mind listens in the background the entire time. It's the conscious mind's job to protect you.

Now, if you find a hypnotist performing his or her act at a festival, you'll most likely find self-help hypnosis recordings for sale at the side table and online. When I was in my early twenties, I bought a hypnosis CD from a brilliant hypnotist I saw perform at the San Diego County Fair. I listened to it every night to help with relaxation and relief from anxiety. There's literally a hypnosis recording for every ailment. These hypnosis recordings are essentially akin to guided meditations that take people into a deeply relaxed hypnotic state that allows their subconscious minds to become open to suggestion. And while in this open state, the hypnotist provides suggestions that align with the topic/ purpose of the recording. For example, in a hypnosis recording related to improving self-esteem, the hypnotist might suggest something along the lines of

> I am a good person.
> I feel good about myself.
> I accept myself.
> I am well respected.
> I have high self-esteem.

With that being said, hypnosis/suggestions may work well as long as there are no underlying issues that are creating the problems for the subject. However, more often than not, there is an underlying issue that must be resolved in order for suggestion therapy to be effective. I work with clients who come in with a perceived problem like anger management. And once we drill down to the root cause(s) of the anger, we discover that the anger is triggered by unresolved childhood trauma. In this case, hypnotic suggestion may only be effective after we've done the hard work of resolving the trauma causing the anger in the first place. That's where hypnotherapy/regression work comes into play.

The word "regression" is defined by the *Oxford English Dictionary* as "a return to an earlier stage of life or a supposed previous life, especially through hypnosis or mental illness, or as a means of escaping present anxieties." In a hypnotic regression, the subject is put into a hypnotic state. Then, the hypnotherapist opens up a safe space where the subject's subconscious mind is free and able to travel back to relive and explore the most relevant memories or experiences causing the unresolved trauma. Once the traumatic memories or experiences have been properly dealt with, then suggestion therapy becomes a much more effective tool.

The Three Primary Types of Regression

There are three primary types of regression practiced in mainstream hypnotherapy:

Current Life Regression: A current life/present life regression is where the hypnotherapist takes a client back to memories or experiences in their current life with the goal of reframing the circumstances that influenced the beliefs, emotions, and behaviors that are problematic for the subject. Then, once regressed back into the relevant memories, the client works to find the understanding and/or closure needed to move forward in a way that serves his or her greatest good.

Past Life Regression: Past life regression is similar to a current life regression except that instead of going to back to memories of an experience in the subject's current lifetime, the subject revisits a past life.

For example, I worked with a client who had a paralyzing fear of death that couldn't be explained by experiences in her current life. After I took my client into a hypnotic trance, she found herself back in a past life where she saw her entire life, including the memory of her tragic and traumatic death. Once she was able to make peace with her death in that previous life, I provided her with hypnotic suggestions that her subconscious accepted. My client no longer fears death.

Past life regression can also help identify karmic issues that have been carried from life to life that need to be addressed. Traveling back to a past life and addressing unresolved issues that have carried over into this lifetime can lead to a beautiful healing. It can also help you better understand the life you're living in this incarnation.

In other words, journeying back to a past life through hypnotic regression may allow you to remember a past life that is most relevant to the current life you're living, find understanding, and move forward in a way that serves your greatest good.

Life Between Lives Regression: Life between lives (LBL) regression, otherwise known as between lives regression, is a deep hypnosis technique developed by psychologist and hypnotherapist Dr. Michael Newton. Dr. Newton spent thirty-five years performing thousands of past-life regressions and discovered that some of his clients were able to reach the "between lives" realm.

Life between lives regression allows us to revisit the places our souls go after the physical body dies and before we reincarnate. Between lives regression allows us to experience our spiritual essence. In an LBL regression, we may experience meeting our guides, loved ones, soul family, or even Source/God.

Additionally, we may gain insight into how we planned our current life before incarnating. LBLs may help provide clarity into why we are here and our current life circumstances.

Many subjects find what I call "soul-level healing" in a life between lives regression. Many find forgiveness for those who have harmed them in their current life. Some begin to understand how the pieces of their lives fit together. And others simply bask in the beauty of what lies beyond the veil.

NDE Regression

In *Back to the Beyond*, we explore a fourth type of regression that I call NDE regression. There has been a very limited amount of research surrounding the regression of NDE experiencers back to their out-of-body experience.

My process for regressing the participants in this research is very similar to how I regress people for current life, past life, and between lives regression. First, I take my clients into a hypnotic state of relaxation. This is known as a hypnotic induction. Then, I take my clients through a meditative visualization, which brings them into a deeper state of hypnosis known as a deepener. The only difference with the NDE regression is the technique I use within the induction protocol. This new technique opens up a safe space of consciousness that allows NDEers to access the experiences and memories most beneficial to receiving closure and peace related to their near-death experience.

Local vs. Nonlocal Memory

Where do memories live? In our brains? In our subconscious minds? The truth is, nobody really knows. Of course, scientists, doctors, psychologists, hypnotherapists, and other experts in the field who do not have strong spiritual leanings are more likely to discount any theory that involves nonlocal memory. In other words, they believe that all memory resides within the brain.

I have had many personal experiences, such as the out-of-body experience shared earlier in the OBE section, that have convinced me that we are so much more than our physical selves. In addition to being a certified hypnotherapist, I'm also a Reiki Master Teacher who uses a variety of energy healing modalities to help my clients heal. Those of us who practice energy healing or are highly intuitive understand the energetic properties of our meridians, chakras, and the energetic body layers that make up our aura (including the astral body mentioned in chapter I). I believe that our past life and between lives memories are stored in our auras/energetic body, which are then channeled into our brains to process when we are under hypnosis, in meditation, having dreams, etc. I also believe that our brain stores memories locally from our current life and our energy body stores them nonlocally. Think about saving a file on your computer's hard drive while also uploading it to a cloud-based app like Dropbox. When your brain eventually dies, you don't lose your memories because they've been stored in the "cloud." And this "cloud" travels with you into the afterlife and with each incarnation you live.

Now, there are hypnotherapists who believe that past life and between life memories are not real memories of past or between lives. These professionals believe that what we experience in a regression is simply our subconscious mind telling us highly believable stories that allow us to work through our unresolved trauma. If this is your belief, I totally respect it. However, please consider the following. There are people who are able to substantiate their past life regression/memories with hard facts and proof. In the introduction of the book, I wrote about a three-year-old boy who remembered his past life, was able to locate his dead body, and then identified the man who killed him (Global Heart, 2017). If the memories of the boy's past life were simply convincing stories that his subconscious mind put together, how did his memories help find someone else's dead body and ID the murderer? I wonder what the odds are that a three-year-old boy's made-up story would end up being 100 percent accurate about someone else's death, place of burial, and who the murderer was. There is a philosophical principle called "Occam's razor," and here's how it works. Suppose two explanations for an occurrence exist. Occam's razor says that the explanation which requires the smallest number of assumptions is the most logical choice. So, if we put Occam's razor in practice against the story of the three-year-old boy who remembered his past life, we have two options:

- The boy recalled memories of a real past life.
- The boy's subconscious mind told a brilliantly vivid made-up story that somehow led authorities to find a random person's dead body and killer.

Which is the simplest theory?

Multidimensional Aspects of the Mind

In order to experience psychic phenomenon, nonlocal memories from a past or between life, and a variety of other "mystical" experiences, we must tap into dimensions outside of the physical realm. And I believe that our brains can act as the connection between the physical and the nonphysical. So, how does the brain do it?

One of the best explanations I've heard is what I refer to as the "Brain Receiver Model." Imagine that your brain is a radio. Now, your radio either has a dial or a tuner that allows you to change the station it's playing. For most of us, we are typically tuned into the human channel/earth plane. Call it the beta brainwave channel. And we stay in the beta brainwave because our ego and conscious mind are constantly talking to us. Our brains are constantly filled with chatter and thoughts. And that activity keeps our attention and awareness locked in on the beta brainwave channel. I liken it to listening to your favorite song. When my jam comes on, you better not touch that dial.

Now, there are tools that can help us change our brain's channel/wave. One technique is through listening to binaural beats with our eyes closed. One of my favorite binaural beats meditation resources is Dr. Eben Alexander's audiobook *Seeking Heaven*. Binaural beats meditation uses sound to bring our brains into alpha, delta, and theta states. Plant medicines, psychedelics, meditation, and hypnosis are other ways to change our brain's channel. Our brains also switch channels as our brain waves change throughout the various sleep cycles. There are a variety of different ways to change the brain's primary active channel to another. And once we've changed our brain's channel from the beta channel to another, we open ourselves up to receiving information from nonphysical dimensions. In other words, your brain waves influence what dimensions you're able to access.

For the research in this book, I used hypnosis to guide the participants out of the beta brainwave and into a frequency that allowed them to reconnect with the realms they visited while out of body during their NDE. What surprised me the most about the research you're about to read from chapter IV on is that, in many cases, the subjects did not regress back to the exact memory of their NDE. Rather, they regressed or progressed (however you want to phrase it) to a dimension that reconnected them with the entities, beings, and experiences they had during their NDE. Access to these dimensions helped participants receive answers not only to the questions they had about their NDE, but also to questions related to their purpose or other important areas of their current life they wished to explore.

CHAPTER IV

JUDY

J udy is a delightful soul who resides in New Zealand. I met Judy after posting a call for NDE regression volunteers in a near-death experience Facebook group. Shortly after the post went live, Judy reached out privately and expressed interest in participating.

During our first conversation, Judy shared that during her near-death experience, she met Jesus, which was curious to her because she wasn't "religious." She didn't believe in Jesus prior to her NDE nor did she feel compelled to the Christian faith after she returned to her body. Judy had always wondered why Jesus appeared in her NDE and wished to explore that during the regression. Additionally, Judy was interested in learning more about the intuitive gifts and abilities that manifested after her NDE. Finally, Judy shared that post NDE, she'd been making contact with extraterrestrial beings and wished to explore that connection in more depth. Judy's account covers a lot of ground and I think you'll find her NDE story and regression fascinating.

Judy's NDE Account

Judy: I'm Judy, and in 2009, I was pregnant with my daughter and at twenty-four weeks, presented with preeclampsia quite severe at that stage. My blood pressure was going through the roof. So they hospitalized me, and I spent the next two weeks in the hospital until she was born, which was twenty-six weeks and two days.

And in those weeks leading up to her being brought out of me, I started to get sicker and sicker and sicker and ended up having what they call HELLP syndrome. This happens when your organs begin to shut down and, in particular, my liver shut down. It was like being in a car accident and having had a big bang against my liver. And my liver developed, for lack of a better word, a hematoma, which is like a bruise. And then that bruise slowly leaked out into my stomach region. And it was extremely painful. And you get referred pain as well, which I got up into my neck and shoulder. And I was getting more and more ill leading up to that twenty-six-week mark. Before that—about a couple of days before that—I didn't realize I was ill. I was a bit in la-la land really. Not in that I wasn't conscious or anything like that, but I was a bit naive. I didn't realize how sick I was. I felt fine. I thought I was fine and I was in the ward by myself. They put me by myself because they wanted complete quiet for me and rest, and the whole idea is to keep the baby in as long as possible to give the baby the greatest chance, while also keeping you healthy and balanced as well. But, unfortunately, they left me too long.

And so, yes, then I started getting HELLP syndrome and it all went to custard really. But before that I was in this ward by myself. It was the middle of the night and I was asleep and I woke up.

And I saw—I call them shadow people. I would say this is probably the first shadow person I ever saw. Yeah, the first shadow person I ever saw was my great-aunt Eleanor. My great-aunt Eleanor and I had never met. I'd seen photographs of her and heard stories about her, and I've always thought that she and I would have gotten on really well. We had lots of things in common—lots of similar interests and things like that. And I always thought, "Wow, she's a lovely lady!" And I often had her photo around my flat and things like that because I just thought she was really cool and beautiful. And yes, I just knew it was her. Like I woke up (silence), I thought—it's like that feeling, you know, when someone's walked in the room. You just know someone's there. And I thought it was a nurse at first and then I saw her and she looked like a shadow. I think I've heard other people talk about seeing spirits before as well and they will look like a shadow. You don't see their features, but you have a knowing and I just knew it was her. And I said to myself, 'It's Eleanor!' And this amazing feeling of calm and tranquility, mostly calm, came over me. I just knew that everything was going to be fine. She was there to tell me that everything would be fine.

And so I just had this incredible calm. And from there on everything got worse and worse and worse medically. I was very calm, and the medical staff couldn't understand why I was so calm, but I just felt quite chilled out about it all. I was like very accepting of everything that was happening.

So, further down the track, they kept trying to control my blood pressure and things like this. I got sicker and sicker and they took me down to the birthing unit, and it was very much any day now that they were going to take my baby, and they were trying to sort of balance the whole thing. And I had this shooting pain.

And that was when the midwife, young midwife, said to them that I was in a bad way and they needed to hurry up and do something. But they still left me (laughter) because they didn't realize what was happening. And then, in my side—my right side—where my liver was so, so sore and it was hard; all my belly had gone hard. And the next day they were like, "Right, we're taking this baby, Judy." And from there, they got me into the emergency room. Once in the ER, I was just completely chilled out, absolutely chilled, and they got me on the table, and it was very painful moving me onto the table.

And they didn't tell me at the time, but the nurse said later that she was a bit concerned about that. She thought that's not normal. And they tried to get the epidural in and I couldn't . . . Normally people sit up and bend over, but I couldn't and so I sort of tried lying on my side and bent as much as I could. That was quite painful—them trying to put the epidural in. And then, finally, it was a go and I was all numb and it was all good to go.

I was still completely chilled out, going with it all, and the next minute, I saw the surgeon's eyes and I could see her eyes over the top of her mask and she was worried. Like she was—I could see she was a bit panicked and I heard her say, "There's all blood in here, there's all blood in here.

And then they brought my daughter, Evelyn, out and sorted her out and then tried to show her to me, but I never saw her. They thought they'd shown her to me but I didn't see her. So they were like, "Look, you see your daughter, Judy?!" and everything started like speeding up. They were rushing and I could tell they were rushing and I just knew something was wrong. And I wasn't bothered by it, but I just knew something wasn't quite right. And they said, "Would you like your husband to stay with you?

Or would you like him to go with your daughter?" And I said, "I think he should go with my daughter," because I just knew something was about to happen and that he shouldn't see that. And so off he went and like he literally walked out the door and the whole room filled up with all these people and they're all talking at a great rate of knots and I was just lying there and then they said to me, "Judy, we need to open you up. Is that okay?" And I thought well what can I do? I can't see anything. You know, I can't say no. So I was like, yeah, that's fine. You know, I was really chilled out about it. And so they opened me up further. And then this is the not very pleasant part. The surgeon, the liver surgeon was up inside me packing my liver out. So what they have to do is pack your liver in order to stop the bleeding first. And then they have to go back later, a day or so, and take the packing out and make sure that it stopped the bleeding. And then they put like a lacquer— almost like a Glad Wrap layer—of glue over the top of your liver and they try and re-create it. And then my liver had to you know, slowly heal itself which took a long time.

And so he was up inside me, and at the time I went with it, but it has played on in my mind, and in hindsight, it was quite traumatic actually. Feeling him up inside me, and he was rough, too, so it wasn't pleasant. And then I got to a point where I was like going with it and I was going to my happy place and just thinking, "Go with it. Go with it." And then I said to the anesthetist that I'd had enough and she said, "Yeah, I think we'll put you under."

And then after that, I don't remember anything apart from waking up in the ICU. I woke up, and the feeling that I had was as though I was close to my body, but I wasn't in my body. I wasn't hovering above it. I wasn't seeing things from that point of view, but I was not fully in my body. I felt like I was sort of in the in-between, but still sort of attached to my body. And I saw my parents and they were standing at the side of the bed and I just felt this love for my parents—we all love our parents. But I just felt this like "all the love in the world" feeling. I've never felt love like that before for my parents. It was incredible. And I wanted to convey that to them, and I was giving it to them, and I was trying to reassure them and comfort them and, unbeknownst to me, I was actually speaking to them. But I don't remember talking to them. And I just remember trying to, you know, convey love to them and show them how much I love them and the feeling that I had around that. And then I'm just trying to remember, I think when I last spoke to you, Adam, I talked also about waking up in the ICU with the tube down my throat and that was quite traumatic as well. I didn't like that. I had a lot of problems with that afterwards. So I pulled it out myself because I thought I was choking, and it was like coming back from down a long tunnel when I came back. It felt like I could hear the nurse and she was way off in the distance speaking to me. That's what it felt like and I felt that I was choking and I just pulled this tube out and I heard her laugh. She must have thought it was a bit funny. But, yeah, and then I just remember being really confused when I woke up. Like where was I? I didn't have any attachment to New Zealand or where I live. I had no memory where I was in terms of place, but I knew who I was, and the first thing I was thinking about was my family and Carl, my husband. And I was, like, asking,

"Where's my husband? Where's Carl?" And I was really confused. Like where is he?

And she said, "Oh, he's gone home." And she said, "Do you want to talk to him?"

I said, "Yes, I do" and she said, "Oh, well, I'll ring him for you."

But I couldn't remember any phone numbers. So the only phone number I could remember was my parents. So I rang my dad in the middle of the night, well, he's the one that picked up. And I said to him,

"How are you?" and the whole time I was asking everybody how they were. "Are you okay? Are you all right?" I wasn't even thinking about myself. So, I got Carl's phone number and I spoke to him and it was all good.

But I have this memory from while I was dead or unconscious. I remember this person/man/being with me. I don't remember seeing it. I saw nothing—I felt it. So it was like a feeling. And it was a black space but not dark and scary; it felt warm, inviting, and all encompassing—like home. And it felt—instead of pitch-black—it felt more like a soft black. And it felt great, felt really good, and I knew that I knew everything. I had all this knowledge.

I knew how the world ticked. I knew how things were just supposed to be and that there was no attachment whatsoever to my body. I never even thought about my body. I never thought about what had happened in the hospital. Nothing. And this man, he felt like a man to me, was with me and he felt paternal and brotherly and very down-to-earth—but of course he wasn't down-to-earth because we were outside of earth (laughing). But he felt really . . . just like regular. Like a regular person. I don't know how to describe this. I didn't feel like I had to adore him and praise him and worship him. That's how he felt. Like my father or my brother. He felt like me, you know? He felt, yeah, so very brotherly and fatherly, and it was beautiful to feel the love. The love was incredible and I just felt like I was home.

And I don't even remember him talking to me. And this is one of the things that I would like to connect with. I would like to know what was said. He did show me pictures though. Almost like a movie of my husband and my daughter and what life would be like for them without me. And how they would go on and that things wouldn't always be easy for them. And it wouldn't be perfect and it wouldn't all go beautifully. But I also saw that it wouldn't be all bad either and that they would just have a different life without me in it. So it wouldn't be a bad thing or a good thing. It was just different. A different life experience for them. And I had this huge understanding of that and this huge acceptance and this feeling of, "That's just the way it is. It's just supposed to be and it's okay." That it was just completely okay. Regardless of what happens, that's okay. Yeah, I felt completely accepting of it. And then I just remember waking up in the ICU.

I was about five days in the ICU and it's all very cloudy. I didn't know how many surgeries I'd had. But I was awake and Carl, my husband, was sitting beside me, and I was just lying there. I was a bit confused about where I was. I thought I was in England because all the staff were Scottish and English (laughter), and I thought I was in England and I said to my husband,

"Am I in England?"

And he said, "No, you're not in England." and I was a little bit confused about where I was. Because I felt that I'd been to a whole other place. And so I was just not connected to the fact that I lived in New Zealand and where I was and things like that.

I felt like my stomach was wide open. I felt like they hadn't closed me up and that it was wide open to the world and it didn't distress me. I just thought I'm wide open.

And then I felt this woman. So again, it's like, you just know someone's walked in the room and they're standing beside you. I didn't see anything, but I felt her and I knew she was a woman and I said to my husband,

"There's a woman here."

And he said, "No. There's no one here."

And I said, "Yeah, there's a woman here."

And then she sat down on my bed next to me, and I felt the compression of her sitting on the bed. And she felt like a slightly larger woman. Like she had quite a large bum for one person. But it felt nice and I said,

"Yeah, yeah, she's just sat down on the bed."

And my husband said, "No, there's no one here."

I said, "Yeah!" And then I felt her touch my stomach and it was like just a really light compression. Like a little. Just a light touch. And from that touch, like when a droplet falls in a pool and there's a ripple outward effect. That's what it felt like. Like there was a ripple outward effect right across my stomach. Right out. And it felt cool like a beautiful cool liquid feeling. And it felt really nice, like it was heaven on a stick. It felt so good on my stomach. And I feel personally that that was a healing. From a higher being. I don't know who they were.

Then, all of a sudden, I said to my husband,

"You know, she's just touched my stomach."

And he said, "No. No one's touched you, Judy. No one's here." And then I felt this presence at the foot of my bed. And in my mind's eye, I can kind of see this. It's really hard because you think you're making these things up, but in my mind's eye, I saw this white light type effect. But I didn't actually see it, so it's very hard to believe it's there. And then I felt this overwhelming feeling like this huge massive wave came right at me and over and down me and it just went, "Boom!" And it was all the love in the world. That's what it felt. Like all the love in the world. It was the most incredible thing.

I said to my husband. "Oh, Jesus is here. Jesus is here."

And he said, "No, Judy. No one's here. No one's here."

I said yeah. "Yeah, he's here. Jesus is here!"

And it just was the most incredible feeling I've ever had in my life. And he wasn't just there for me. He was there for everyone. Full force. And I just knew it was Jesus and I am not religious. I am not a religious person. I haven't been brought up religious. For me to say that I have met God or met Jesus is uncomfortable for me. I've had to do a long journey of coming to grips with it and getting comfortable with it. And I don't think I'm even still fully comfortable with it. Because for me growing up—well, honestly, my brothers would make fun of people that believed in God and believed in Jesus, and we were happy for other people to do that. It was sort of scoffed at by my family. So, I have found that really difficult to know that I've had this amazing experience with Jesus, and I know I met him. I just know in my heart. And I've struggled with that experience. Believing fully in it. It hasn't made me want to be religious thereafter. I would more call myself spiritual. And I do talk to him and I do believe he's with me and all those things, but I don't feel the need to go to church or praise him or worship him. It's not that kind of relationship. It's like I'm still talking to my brother or I'm talking to my father. That's how I feel about it.

And so yeah, so he turned up and it was incredible. And there were two other people in the ICU at the time. There was a man beside me in the bed who was dying. I saw his ancestors coming for him. There were so many. And they were shadow people. It was overwhelming because I could feel everything. It was a bit scary actually. And he was a Maori man. And so his people that were there for him were praying over him in Maori, and it was very overwhelming because I could feel that he had not been a terribly good person in life. He'd done some bad things. And I could feel that they had a sadness. His ancestors felt a sadness. And they were going to have to take him through to the other side—I'm having a difficult time thinking of the words to describe it—he was going to have to do a review of what he'd done in life and how he behaved and who he'd hurt and things like that. I don't know how that would be, but that's what it felt like, and it felt uncomfortable and I didn't handle that very well. I was probably a bit rude (laughter), because it felt so intense to me and so dense and so really sort of like the energy felt so dense, and it's not my culture personally. I was a bit kind of scared and confused and I out loud said "Please shut up. Please shut up; please stop praying. Please stop doing that because it feels so uncomfortable."

And then there was a little baby in the other bed beside me—and in a bad way. And I could hear her. And I knew that she was going to be okay, that she was going to live. And that Jesus was there for her too, and he was helping with her as well. So it was really amazing. It was mind-blowing for someone who is not religious. I just couldn't believe that I'd had this experience—and at the time I was fully in it. It was Jesus. That was it. I was not questioning it. I was fully in it. But further on, as time went on, I told people about it. So I told my parents about it, and I talked more with my husband about it. My mom said to me, "It's really weird that you're still going on about that, Judy, because when we came to see you in the ICU, you were saying to me over and over 'Jesus is here, Mom. It's okay. Jesus is here. It's all right. Everything's going to be fine. Everything's going to be fine. Don't worry. Jesus is here." And so the fact that I was still talking about this afterwards when I was in the surgical ward—they were quite surprised that I've talked about it ever since. I did go through a stage of not talking about it, because I thought people were a bit freaked out about it.

Also, since then, I have started to be able to talk to people who have passed over. They give me messages for their loved ones, though not all the time. I can't turn it on. I can't like switch it on, but it'll just happen randomly. And at the start, the spirits who communicated with me were always a connection that I knew. I might have either met them briefly or they were a distant relative or something like that. And then, as time went on, it was people I had never met in my life coming to give me a message for someone. That was really amazing and took a bit of getting used to.

And then I had people who hadn't passed on who had Alzheimer's, dementia, and cancer come to me before they passed on or while they were still in that ill state, and give me messages for their loved ones, which blew my mind. And then I started to have other experiences that have also blown my mind. So, this is also so hard for me to talk about, but I've met star beings. In my meditations, I've met one of my guides who is a celestial star being. I guess it's what they call them. I've also had, in the last year, denser experiences. So I've been helping people who have been not very good people in life or who have committed suicide and they're stuck. Or they feel remorse about what they've done in their lives. I've helped them pass over and meet the people they're supposed to meet and move on to the next stage of going through being accountable for what they've done and getting them to come to grips with that. They would have to go through that in order to move forward.

I've unfortunately picked up a bit of a dark energy when I went to a hotel recently and I had an experience with needing to clear that and get rid of that. I thought I was only ever going to have light, nice experiences because I had met Jesus and it was all going to be lovely and I was only going to meet like, you know, really light souls. But I have started to meet these souls that are a little bit more tormented. I've had so many different experiences, and each soul is so different, and how they handle their death. Or how they're dying, or how they handle being over on the other side. How they feel about it and how they're processing it. It is different. So I'm always surprised when a lot of people say, "Oh they're always at peace, they're always happy over there." They aren't always, in my experience. Some of them struggle with it. Some of them need help processing it. And they go through a process as well, and I've watched it and seen it. There are some souls that are serene and content and at peace, and it's beautiful and they're very accepting. And others struggle with it. They might have been murdered or took their own life and thought it was going to be better after, but they're still stuck. Still stuck with the darker feelings. So there has been a massive learning curve and a journey that I'm still on. And yeah, it's been interesting. It's been hard but interesting and that's about it.

After we concluded recording Judy's NDE account, Judy and I discussed what she wanted to cover during her regression session.

- When my NDE began, I experienced being in a soft, dark space. And in that space, I met a paternal/brotherly type of being. Who was that being?

- Regarding the woman who touched my stomach which led to the beautiful liquid feeling, who was she? And why did she come?

- Questions for Jesus:

  - Why did he come to me since I don't believe in him?

  - What is my relationship supposed to be with Jesus?

- What did we discuss when I met you during the NDE?
- What are my spiritual gifts/abilities?
- What is the purpose of my life?
- Who are the star beings? And why are they making contact with me?
- Why is it that I have crippling self-doubt?

In our regression session, I took Judy into a hypnotic state and then set the intention for her to experience whatever serves her soul's greatest good as it related to her NDE. The following is a transcript of Judy's regression session.

Judy's NDE Regression

I facilitated Judy's NDE regression a week after she shared the account of her near-death experience. Judy arrived to the Zoom session excited to revisit her NDE and find the closure she sought. I spent approximately ten minutes getting Judy into a deeply relaxed hypnotic trance. Once Judy was in a hypnotic trance, I asked her to use her powerful imagination to visualize a hallway with many doors, with each of the doors representing an experience or a set of memories from her life. I then asked Judy to find a door that seemed to stand out from the others and walk up to it. Once Judy arrived at the door, she said, "I'm here." Then, I connected Judy with the intention that we set for the regression and asked her to walk through the door. Below is a verbatim transcription of Judy's regression session.

Judy walks through the door—

Adam:
Judy, tell me your impression. What are you seeing?

Judy:
Nothing. I don't see anything. It's just really warm.

Adam:
Okay, good.

Judy:
I feel warm. (Silence)

Judy:
It's more of a feeling. I feel stuff, but I can't see. (Silence)

Judy:
I see gold. I see colors.

Adam:
Okay, great.

Judy:
Colors, goldy colors. Everything is quite murky.

Adam:
Okay, that's great. You're doing just fine. I want you to go ahead and look down at your feet. Can you tell if you're wearing anything on your feet?

Judy:
No. No. I have bare feet.

Adam:
Okay, bare feet. Excellent.

Judy:
I'm floating. I'm floating.

Adam:
Okay, wonderful. Do you get a sense for where you may be floating? Does it feel like anywhere in particular?

Judy:
Like a high. I can't even describe it. Like a nothingness, but a nice nothingness. I don't know how to describe it. It's got pinks and golds and there's black in there too, but it's like a charcoaly sort of black, and I'm just floating. I'm just floating.

Adam:
That's great. That's great. Do you get the sense if any beings are nearby or in your vicinity?

Judy:
Yeah, the father is there. The father. He's white. Really unusual looking. Almost Egyptian looking, but white. White, white, white, white. With

the most amazing blue eyes I've ever seen in my life. They're just like sapphires. Very friendly. I feel like he's my father. He's got long white hair. He's floating. He's floating as well. And he's got a weird shaped body, so a really long neck. He's just there. He's not saying anything. I feel really good.

Adam:
Good. Good. Judy, do you want to ask this fatherly figure who he is?

Judy:
Someone else is— *(Silence)*

Judy:
Oh, God. I want to cry.

Adam:
It's okay, go ahead. This is your safe space, Judy. Go ahead and just—

Judy:
I know that it's Jesus. It's Jesus.

Adam:
Good.

Judy:
They're both there. It's intense. We're just floating in the space, and there's little sparkly lights. Really intense. *(Silence)*

Adam:
Are you able to ask the fatherly figure who he is?

Judy:
I can't hear anything.

Adam:
Okay, so he's not answering?

Judy:
No.

Adam:
Okay, that's fine. And Jesus is still there?

Judy:
He just said, "You know who I am. You know who I am. You know me, Judy. You know me. I'm your people. You've come from us and we are you and you are us. You're my daughter. You're my daughter. You're my daughter." And Jesus is just, he's just there.

Adam:
He's just hanging out?

Judy:
Yeah, he's not saying anything.

Adam:
That's okay. We're going to talk to Jesus in a few minutes.

Judy:
Okay.

Adam:
Before we get into the questions, take a look around at where you are. What does it look like? What are you experiencing right now?

Judy:
All these colors. I'm not in a place. It's like a space. Just lots of colors and these little fine twinkly lights. They're like stars. They look like stars, but they're kind of blinking on and off. They're just really beautiful. Really galaxy-like. Yeah, and it's just this color. The pink is beautiful, and there's blue, and it's all merged like a color palette. It's all wishy-washy. There's a sort of black there too, like this soft gray black. And behind this guy, this father, is people. Is more of him. But they're off to my right side, and Jesus is off to my left.

Adam:
That's wonderful.

Judy:
Jesus is just smiling. He's just smiling, like he has a big knowing.

Adam:
That's great. Judy, does this place feel familiar? Does it feel strange? How does it feel to you?

Judy:
Familiar.

Adam:
Okay. Okay.

Judy:
This is home. This is my home.

Adam:
Mm-hmm (affirmative).

Judy:
But it's not fully there yet.

Adam:
Okay.

Judy:
I'm not fully there yet.

Adam:
That's okay.

Judy:
I'm just sort of not quite where I belong.

Adam:
So Judy, that sort of darker space, that charcoaly space that you're seeing, in your near-death experience you shared that you saw a soft, dark space. Is it a similar soft darkness that you're seeing there, or is it different?

Judy:
Yeah, it's the same.

Adam:
Okay.

Judy:
Yeah. It's sort of, like, out of focus.

Adam:
Okay.

Judy:
Yeah.

Adam:
I want you to think about that soft, dark space and connect with it in any way that you feel inclined to connect. Now, you mentioned that you met a paternal and brotherly type of being. Did you want to ask the father or Jesus or any of the other beings present, who that person was? Who that being was?

Judy:
The Holy Spirit. That's what I heard. It's really faint. The Holy Spirit. Weird. I'm not religious. I don't believe in that.

Adam:
That's okay. You're doing wonderful. Just keep letting it flow.

Judy:
The Holy Spirit.

Adam:
What was the reason for the Holy Spirit coming to you, in that moment?

Judy:
To help me. To help me to grow and expand. To nurture me. To guide and to show me where I come from, what I can do. What I can do for others. Who I am. To give me some knowledge and others. (Silence)

Judy:
Shape. Shape, something about it shaping something.

Adam:
Something about what?

Judy:
Shaping the future. Shaping the future generation. And something to do with my son and my daughter. Shaping future generations. Shaping, changing. Changing and shaping and cutting ties and cutting chains. Cutting ways of being. Cutting ways of being. Oh God. Being around him is really intense. (Silence)

Adam:
I'm sure. Judy, while you're there, why don't you ask the Holy Spirit to enter into your body and provide whatever love and energy that your body needs at this moment? Just invite it in. And just feel it. You're doing great. (Silence)

Do you want to ask if there is anything you don't remember, that the Holy Spirit shared with you, while in that moment, that is important for you to know now?

Judy:
Okay. It's showing me, again, what he showed me last time. (Silence)

Judy:
Fragments of Carl and Evelyn. We want you, we want, very faint. We want you to go forward. We want you to go forward. (Silence) Can't hear it. (Silence)

Judy:
Can't hear it.

Adam:
If you can't hear the voice, why don't you ask the Holy Spirit to place the

message in your heart, and maybe you can sense it or feel it? And if you can't, that's okay too.

Judy:
He wants me to help people who are suicidal. People in the dark. People who are in the dark. People in the dark. People in turmoil. Turmoil.

Judy:
So the darkness, the darkness that I see is the darkness that, like a space that they're stuck in. They're stuck in that space. That charcoaly black, they're stuck in that space and they can't get out or move or expand, and they're stuck there. He's showing me it, that that's what it's like. They want me to help them.

Adam:
Those beings who are stuck there, are they still alive? Or are they souls that have crossed over that haven't found their way to the other side?

Judy:
Those are people who could go there, that could get there one day and be stuck in that place as well as people who are over there and stuck in that place.

Adam:
Okay.

Judy:
They're stuck in there. It's not a bad place. It's not a bad place. It's just limbo. It's like a nothing place. It's not horrible, but it's a stuckness. And they're not expanding. They need to expand and move forward. I'm not using the right language. It's an expansion of consciousness. It's not higher or lower than anybody. Nobody's higher or lower. It's an expansion of your being, and that's important because you get stuck. And when you get stuck, you're lost. And you're lost to yourself and who you're meant to be. That's really beautiful. You're lost to yourself and who you're meant to be. Oh God. Oh my God. He's just given me all this love. Whoa, that is amazing.

Adam:
That's beautiful.

Judy:
Oh God, that's so nice.

Adam:
Just enjoy it. Just let it radiate in.

Judy:

He really loves everybody and he just wants everybody to be their best self. Their highest self, and their best self, and to know that they are loved and they are more than what they think they are. This guy, the father's got something to do with it too. The people out there have got something to do with it as well. It's just an expansion. Everything is an expansion. Whoa, amazing.

Adam:

That's beautiful. Do you know what the father and the people, when you say they're part of it, the expansion, do you have any idea what roles they're playing in that?

Judy:

They work together. They work together. They're all a part of it. There's no one higher. They work together. It's a together thing.

Adam:

Okay, that's great.

Judy:

It's something bigger than them. (Silence)

Adam:

There's something bigger present?

Judy:

It's just all around us. It's everywhere.

Adam:

What is it?

Judy:

It encompasses everything. I don't know. It's not a thing. I don't know how to describe it. Like an energy. I don't know how to describe it. It's something I can't pinpoint.

Adam:

Okay.

Judy:

Like a feeling.

Adam:

Okay. Good. Good, you're doing great.

Judy:

We're just a part of it.

Adam:
Judy, is Jesus . . . (Interjected by Judy)

Judy:
I heard cosmic. I don't know what that, I just heard cosmic.

Adam:
That's amazing.

Judy:
I don't know what that means. Cosmic.

Adam:
Don't worry about what that means. Don't analyze it, just let it be.

Judy:
Okay. Cosmic.

Adam:
Just take it for what it is. If you're meant to understand it, you'll get the message.

Judy:
We're all part of the cosmos, that's what they said. We're all part of the cosmos. Cool.

Judy asks, "What's that? I don't know what a cosmos is."

She's shown: It encompasses everything. It's the big thing. It's the big thing.

Adam:
It's a big thing?

Judy:
What people call, that's the thing people call God.

Adam:
Okay.

Judy:
But it's just, it's like a—there's no word for it.

Adam:
How are the Holy Spirit and Jesus connected with this energy?

Judy:
Just a part of it. A consciousness. We are here. We are teachers. We are teachers. We are the teachers. We are the teachers. We teach and grow

and expand you all. We teach and grow and expand you all. We are the teachers.

Adam:
Jesus and the Holy Spirit are? Is that what's being said?

Judy:
Yeah, and this guy Father. They're the teachers to enlighten and lift, enlighten and expand. Know thyself. Know thyself. Know thyself so you know thyself. Know thyself.

Adam:
Mm-hmm (affirmative).

Judy:
Really adamant about it.

Adam:
Okay.

Judy:
Grow. You've got to grow. You've got to grow, and you've got to grow your children. Your children, yeah, and lift them, and heighten them too. They have to be heightened. I don't know why.

Judy asks, "Why?"

Judy hears the answer, "Know thyself. Know thyself."

If we raise—if all of us raise ourselves. Yeah, all of us get raised if we raise ourselves. It's like, cosmic. The cosmos of knowledge and learning and experience. Yeah. Breaking those chains of the past. Yeah. That's cool.

Adam:
So if Jesus is still there, I know one of the questions that you had for him was related to why he came to you since you don't believe that he's God. Did you want to ask him?

Judy:
Yeah. He said, "Why not?"

Adam:
Why not come to you? Or why not believe in him?

Judy:
Just why not come to me? Why not you? Why not you? Why not? What does it matter? It doesn't matter. He's got a grin on his face like he knows everything. Quite funny, like he's got this really good sense of humor. Yeah, why not? Because I love you. Because I love you.

Judy:
Sorry, I've got this connection with this guy, this father. That's a little bit part of it. Something to do with the fact that I'm his daughter. Yeah, and something to do with Owen. Owen, my son.

Judy asks, "Why?"

Judy's answered, "Wanted you to feel, I wanted you to feel it. I wanted you to feel it."

Adam:
Feel what?

Judy:
The magnitude of it. The immensity, magnitude of it.

Judy asks, "Why? Why me? Why me?"

Judy's shown: I'm a creator of change. I'm a creator of change. I create change. I'm a change maker. I'm here to create change. I'm a change maker. I'm a change maker. I'm busting things. I'm busting patterns. There's loads of us. We create change. We change people. We change, let people change and grow. It's all about creating more love, people expanding consciousness, and ending the abuse and knowing themselves. We do that in little, tiny little ways. Little gems. Little gold gems. We just plant them, and we just pot them here and there. They can be really subtle, and we don't even know we're doing it. We just go and we can just plant the gems in places." (Silence)

Judy:
"It can be a passing conversation. It can be a smile."

He said to me my smile lights up, lights people up. People like us are put here for that purpose, to, oh God. To put a light on the dark. I started laughing, I can't help it. I'm sorry. Put a light in the dark. In the dark spaces and places, and to counter it. To counteract the dark. Counteract the dark. It's all about knowing yourself. Isn't it? It's all about knowing yourself. Know thyself. Know yourself. These people are here like me, to sprinkle. He's showing me sprinkling, like golden sprinkles. But it's all golden, like little golden stars, sprinkling them around. Lighting up people's lives. Lighting up parts of their souls.

Judy:
It's a huge, massive, massive part, and we are all interconnected. You have to have lots of us. Lots and lots and lots and lots of us. He's shown me that when things are shifting and changing and people's belief

systems are shifting and changing, you need people like us to sprinkle those little gold nuggets. Like little gold sprinkles. And that lightens and heightens things more and more and more. It's what they want.

Judy asks, "What do they want then?"

Judy's answered, "For the greater good."

Judy responds, "I don't get why this is all necessary."

Judy's shown: Because that makes the encompassing thing better. Like it makes the encompassing thing (silence), stronger is the wrong word. The encompassing thing greater. Stronger is the wrong word, because it's not a power thing. It's better or stronger or greater, but they're not the right words. Makes that encompassing thing even better. Does that make sense?

Adam:
Yep.

Judy:
That's really good. It's a good thing, not a bad thing. A good thing. A good thing for everybody that that encompassing thing is good for everybody. We get caught down in the fogginess. We get caught down in the foggy, murky, foggy, foggy stuff, and that's not what it's all about, and we're stuck in it. We're stuck. We are stuck. Our world is stuck. We're stuck, and they're trying to raise us. That's what that means. They're trying to help us. They are trying to help us, and that's why they're all part of it and working together. They're trying to help us, because we're stuck. We're stuck. Yeah, we're stuck, and we're not going to expand and we're not going to go any, we're just not going to expand and know ourselves fully and truly if we keep getting bogged down in the stuff. It's so, it's like the bottom of the bottom, and we're stuck in it, and we keep doing it. We keep doing the same old. We keep going around and around in circles.

Judy:
We're really young. We're really young. Our world is really young, and it's really young. So they're helping us, because they're ancient. They're really way ahead of us, and we're bogged down.

Adam:
Who is "they?"

Judy:
This father guy, he's like a light. He's like a light being type of a star being type thing. He looks weird. He's got these really long arms. He's like the

whitest. Like a shimmery white. He's got this really long hair, but he's got this really high forehead. He's got these sapphire eyes and this beautiful mouth. His nose, like a really long chin, and he's really loving. Really loving. And there's a lot of him. He comes from a long line. There's loads of them, and there's others too. Others too. It's like he's really skinny and he's got these big feet, and they don't wear very much. Quite Egyptian-like looking. They don't talk. They talk with their heads. Their minds or their heads.

Judy:
Jesus is a more humanistic type. Of course he is, from how he's looking. I don't know. He came here, so yeah. He came here. He's one of us. He's sprinkling the gold, making the change. They're trying to lift us. They're trying to lift the earth. They're trying to lift us. They're trying to lift us up. Yeah.

Adam:
So Judy, you mentioned that there were star beings that were making contact with you. Did you want to ask if they're the ones who have been visiting you?

Judy:
It's the same one. (Silence)

Adam:
Okay, and why are they—(Judy chimes back in)

Judy:
I can't see—I can't see the other ones. I can't see the other ones I've seen.

Adam:
But you sense they're there.

Judy:
Yeah, they're there, but they're right out the back. Right out the back. Yeah.

Adam:
Do you get a sense of why they've been making contact with you? You want to ask?

Judy:
To raise your vibration. To raise your vibration. Hmm. Sounds spiritual. To raise you, raise your consciousness for the work you have to do. The work, you've got work to do. It's not work like, it's not like we think of work. To help me and to, yeah. I'm going to pass it on. Just there. They're

just there. Just their way. Just their way. Just the way they communicate, and the way they—

Judy asks, "Why is it so hard?"

Judy's shown, "Sometimes I fight it. I fight it. I'm fighting it. Gentle. I just see the word gentle. You need to go gentle. I need to be more gentle with myself. Kinder, I need to be kinder to myself. I'm too hard on myself, and I have too high expectations of myself. Accept. I just need to accept." They just keep repeating it. Accept. I need to accept. Okay. (Silence)

Judy:
Judy asks, "Why am I doing this? I don't believe in myself. I don't believe in who I am. Why don't I believe in who I am? Why don't I believe in who I am?"

Judy's shown: It's too big. They're laughing at me. They're laughing their heads off at me. That's funny. They're laughing at me. Not in a horrible way, but . . . nothing bad is going to happen. I'm going to be okay. They've got my back. They want me to expand myself, and I need to be more gentle and just go with it. I don't have to be anything. Go with it.

Judy:
I keep thinking that I had to be this big thing. I had to make stuff happen. They said I don't. I don't have to. Just being here.

Judy asks, "Did I choose to come back?"

Judy's shown: I wasn't given the choice. I've struggled with that, because I didn't get given a choice. I got sent back. I didn't actually get a choice. I've been struggling with it. I've been struggling with that. I didn't expect to come back, so, when I came back, they came back with me to help me, try and help me. That's why he stood at the foot of my bed and they sent someone to heal my tummy because I didn't expect to come back. I wasn't supposed to come back, but they sent me back, so I didn't get a choice.

Adam:
Who is that woman who touched your stomach? The one who came back? Did you want to ask who that was?

Judy:
She's my mother. She's my mother and the father is like a paternal person. And she's my mother. Yeah. Yep. She's my mum and he's my dad.

Adam:
That's beautiful.

Judy:
*Yeah, that's who they are. And Jesus was just sitting there. He was just
helping. He's not the big guru. He just helps. He's a helper. He just kind of
works in the middle, if you know what I mean. He's not higher or greater.
He just helps. He's a helper. They all help each other; that's how it works.
(Silence)*

Adam:
*Judy, I know one of the questions that you wanted to ask was what your
relationship is supposed to be with Jesus now. Do you want to ask what
sort of relationship you're supposed to have with him?*

Judy:
*Okay. He said, "I will help you if you call. I will help you if you need me to."
That's what he told me.*

Adam:
Okay, great.

Judy:
*But I don't have to praise him or, he doesn't care about any of that. That's
nice and lovely and marvelous, but it's like I don't have to do that. He's
just there for me. He just helped me. He'll help wherever he can. He's just
a really cool dude. He's just this really cool person. He's not a person, but
you know what I mean.*

Adam:
Mm-hmm (affirmative). Yeah.

Judy:
*I can't even describe him. He's just so easygoing. That's how I'd put it.
Yeah. He's just there, and if I need him, and if I want him to help me,
he'll help. And I can call on him whenever I need to for some help and
guidance and he'll give it. And he's happy to.*

Adam:
*So Judy, I know one of the things that you were looking to do with this
regression was to learn how to control and turn your spiritual gifts and
abilities on and off at will. Is that something you can ask Jesus to help you
with? Is Jesus, is that something—(Judy chimes in)*

Judy:
So—(Silence)

Judy:
Okay. Can't hear anything. (Silence)

Judy:
I have to figure it out for myself.

Adam:
Okay.

Judy:
Because I have to learn how to tap into it, and I have to learn what works for me. But I'm on my way. Oh, okay. I'm on my way. Okay. I know what he means. I'm on my way, yeah. I know what he's talking about. Gentle, softly, gentle. Yeah, I've been running and rushing at it. I have too. I've been running and rushing at it, and gentle, softly, and I'm on my way. Meditation. It's about slowing everything down. I have to slow everything down, because I've been running and rushing. I just need to chill out. Softly, gently, keep things softly, gently. There's no rush. You don't have to be anything, just let it come.

Adam:
Mm-hmm (affirmative).

Judy:
They're going to show me; we're going to give you bits.

Judy asks, "We're going to give you bits?"

Judy's shown: We're going to give you stuff over time, something like, I don't know. We're going to give you bits. Little bits of knowledge. Little bits of practice over time. We'll get you there, and you don't have to be anything. You just need to be yourself, and when it happens, it happens. And just enjoy. Just enjoy it. That's it. Just enjoy it—enjoy the process. Stop running and rushing at it. Gentle. They want me to go more gently. Stop trying to make it happen. I know what they mean. I've just started doing this. I'm alert to what they're talking about. Just slowing everything down. Stop trying to be what I think I should be, and just be me. That's all I need to be. You know this already. Yep, I do. I wasn't supposed to come back, and they just want me to slow down.

Judy:
I'm sad that I came back. I didn't want to come back. I love my husband and my daughter, but I didn't want to come back. That sucks. They're saying sorry. It's nice. They're trying to fill me with that love to sustain me, because they knew that it was tough. I'm laughing now because they're laughing. They knew it was tough—a tough ask. Man, that's why I saw them going off without me. That's why I saw that, and I was totally fine

with it. Totally fine that they did, that I wasn't going to be in their lives. That's interesting.

Adam:
Judy, totally fine about what?

Judy:
I was totally fine that Carl and Evelyn were not going to have me in their lives.

Adam:
Oh, okay.

Judy:
That's what they showed me. They just showed me that, and I was fine with it. I didn't want to come back. That's why I've been struggling. I have to think. I'm glad I came back. I am really glad I came back. That's why they also gave me Owen, when I left. Because my son, Owen, he's a little gift. I wasn't supposed to have any more children, so they gave me a little gift. Okay. Hmm. I think I want to come back now. I've had enough.

Adam:
Judy, one more thing before you return. You did mention that you have crippling self-doubt. Did you want to ask any of the beings you're with if they wanted to guide you to a memory in this current life that causes you to have crippling self-doubt? So that they can heal that experience?

Judy:
Okay. When I was really small, it was how I was brought up. It was how I was brought up. (Silence)

Adam:
And is there an opportunity to heal from that now? Is there an opportunity, is Jesus, is there any way to heal in this moment, or is this something that you have to work on?

Judy:
I think I have to work on it a little bit. But he put his hand on my heart and he said, "You can let it go. You can let that go." It feels good. Feels real good.

Adam:
Good. Just allow that feeling to resonate through your body, Judy.

CHAPTER V

JONNY

J onathan Rizzo is a dear friend of more than twenty years. In 2009, Jonny contracted H1N1 and pneumonia that was so severe that his doctors induced him into a coma. While in the comatose state for twenty-one days, Jonny had a remarkable near-death experience. Jonny documents his full NDE story in his book *Three Hours to Live*, which is a must-read.

In the following NDE account and subsequent regression, Jonny spent most of his time with Jesus. And Jonny experienced Jesus as many Christians do—as Lord and Savior. Jonny's account is the only account in this book to have experienced Jesus as accounted for in the New Testament. Additionally, Jonny's is the only account in this book where a participant experienced visiting hell in the NDE. One of the most beautiful outcomes of Jonny's NDE regression is that the fear left over from his hell experience was remediated.

Finally, I would like to dedicate this chapter of *Back to the Beyond* to Jonny's mother, Teresa Rizzo, who left her body two weeks before we recorded Jonny's NDE account.

Jonny's NDE Account

PART I

Jonny: So I'm Jonny Rizzo, I'm thirty-six years old, and I'm going to share a story of something that happened to me ten to eleven years ago in 2009–2010. I'm born and raised in San Diego. I have a wife of eight years and three daughters. My story goes back to when I was twenty-four years old and I was a part-time youth pastor. I was living in Mission Valley with one of my three best friends in life. And I was working for a university as an enrollment counselor. And it was a Sunday, I remember, and I was feeling pretty crappy, but my friends really wanted me to have dinner with them because one of their family members from New York was in town.

I had a fever of like a 103–104, but I didn't want to let my friends down. So I went to dinner and I was feeling really, really bad after dinner and I didn't tell them I was sick after dinner that night. So, it was a Sunday night and I drove myself to the ER. My father and my then girlfriend at the time met me in the ER and I ended up being there for about six hours or so. And the doctors didn't know what was wrong with me, but I was very ill.

They did a spinal tap for meningitis that came back negative. They did the chest X-ray and there was no sign of pneumonia. So they thought I just had the flu. I took that Monday off, that Tuesday off, that Wednesday off, that Thursday off, and that Friday off, and I was literally just living on my couch in Mission Valley. My sister Sara came down on Wednesday halfway through that week, and I was too weak. Too weak to even get up off the couch. So she had to let herself in and she brought me soup, and she realized how ill I was. She called my mom and dad and said, "Hey, you guys need to pick Jonny up and let him recover at your house. He's not doing too well."

So my dad picked me up on Wednesday, probably around noon, and brought me back to my parents' house. I ended up spending the night.

On Thursday night, my mom waited on me like a nurse. I mean, every three minutes she was checking on me. And by Friday, my condition had not improved and I had lost a little bit of weight. So we went to my family doctor who was about ten minutes from my parents' house. After examining me, the doctor said I had bronchitis, possible pneumonia, and that I would get better by just resting and drinking fluids. By Saturday, my condition did not improve.

It was July 26, 2009. My life would change forever. It was about 3:00–3:30 in the morning. I woke up in my sister's old room and I could barely breathe. And when I say, "barely breathe," I was literally gasping for air. I walked out of the bedroom and turned left into the bathroom upstairs. I turned on the light and I was spitting up a lot of blood. And that commotion woke up my parents. And my mom and dad came in, and they said, "Let's go to the hospital. They'll probably hook you up to an IV. You're probably dehydrated and we will be home in a few hours."

My little brother, Alex, was nine or ten at the time. He was at church camp and my mom or dad had to be there to pick him up. So my mom stayed back and me and my dad went to the emergency room at Grossmont Hospital in La Mesa, California. My dad and I got to the ER around 4:10 AM and it's a circular emergency drop-off and he dropped me off and he went to park the car. So, I walked into the hospital by myself, signed the forms and everything. They gave me a wheelchair because I was in really bad shape. And they instantly took me back because they realized that I was really, really bad. And so they took me to the back and within ten to fifteen minutes of showing up at the ER, I was put into an induced coma. A drug-induced coma that the doctors put me in. And within ten to fifteen minutes of being put into a coma, the hospital room—the ER—was, as I describe in my book, pure chaos. But it was also, the way I described it, like a movie where the person who's having the experience, the way that they're viewing everything is kind of like slow motion. Like when the movie turns black and white and it's just like this slow motion going on. It was chaos, but it was a slow-motion chaos.

I had four doctors. I had nurses coming in and out like crazy and they were drawing blood, doing X-rays, etc. And I say this when I speak to groups about my experience, because people need to know the severity of the situation. Me and my dad were super confused. Didn't know what was going on. We thought it was going to be a simple, "Hook him up to an IV and we'll get home in a couple hours." Then we met Dr. Fox, Dr. Dale Fox. Dr. Fox is the best doctor I've ever known. And he looked at me and my dad and he said, "If this was my son, I'd be scared shitless." And people are like, oh a doctor shouldn't talk like that, but he was letting us know the severity of the situation. It ended up being swine flu, H1N1, which was going around in 2009. And when they knocked me into the coma, my SO2, which is, if you go to the doctor, they put a little machine on your finger and it tells you what your oxygen level is. And mine was 47 percent and dropping about a percent a minute.

So, they made the decision to put me in a drug-induced coma, and I don't remember this part. Well, I remember I called my girlfriend at the time. It was about, I don't know, 4:10 or 4:20 in the morning. I pulled my phone out and I was laying back in the ER. And I remember I was wearing white-and-black-striped shoes. I remember the shorts I was wearing and I was wearing a white T-shirt, and I pulled out my phone and I said,

"Hey." I woke her up in a deep sleep.

I said, "Hey, I'm not going to be able to talk to you for a couple days."

And before I could even say, "I love you," the phone was yanked out of my hand and the doctor said, "You're wasting time." So, I gave the phone to my dad and they kicked him out of the room. And that was the last thing I remember. I laid my head back and/or I laid my arms back and I was lying flat, but they kicked my dad out.

And I prayed. I just said, "God this is it. I'm twenty-four. It sounds like I'm about to die. I don't want to die. But if this is it, forgive me for my sins. I'm ready to meet you blah blah blah." I said, "Amen," and the peace that surpasses all understanding came literally from my head and it filtered down to my toes. It was kind of like a rush. Like an ocean rush that just started at the top and ended at the bottom.

And then I don't remember anything else, but my dad said he could hear from outside the door that the doctors were screaming at me. He could hear them saying, "Open your mouth! Open your mouth!" because they were trying to put a ventilator down my throat—which I don't remember. Thank God. All I remember was saying, "Amen" in my prayer and that was it. I ended up being in a coma for three weeks on life support, full life support for three weeks. I was in the hospital from July 26 to August 24, so thirty days total that I was in the hospital.

I spent twenty-five days in the ICU. I spent twenty-one days in a coma. Twenty-five days in an ICU. And five days in recovery on the fifth floor. I would end up spending the next fourteen months in rehab and recovery. In rehab, I learned how to talk, write, spell, and think. Basically, I was a newborn in a twenty-four-year-old body trying to learn how to live.

While I was in the coma, if you read the doctor's reports, which is literally—and I'm not exaggerating—my hospital paperwork was close to five hundred pages because the notes are very detailed. In the first couple of pages, Dr. Fox was talking about knocking me out. And they use what's called Propofol, which is known as the Michael Jackson drug. That's what he died of. And the doctor's notes literally say, "He was like a horse being put to sleep and my body was rejecting the medicine," and the only option for me to live was to put me into the coma and the only option they had was to put me under using Propofol. And in the doctor's notes they said they gave me four times the appropriate amount because my body kept rejecting it and they thought that I was going to die of an overdose from the Propofol. But that was the only option they had and obviously I survived.

The first seven days that I was in the coma, it was touch-and-go. The first seven days, every night, they sat my family down and said,

"He's not going to live through the night. Prepare his funeral."

And then I would live and then they would say, "He's not going to live through the night." And then I lived and they'd say, "All right. Well, he's not going to live tonight—prepare his funeral." And that happened for seven days.

My older brother, a doctor, flew in from Ohio on the same day that I went to the hospital. So I went in that Sunday morning. He was there by nighttime and he went in and looked at my charts and talked with the doctors and he came out and said, "Mom and Dad, he's not going to live. There's no way he can live." They put me in what's called a RotoProne bed, which is also known as a pronation bed. And it's called proning, where they put you on your back and on your stomach. It's a three- to four-hundred-thousand-dollar bed and the hospital did not have it. They had a contract for the bed, but they hadn't used it in fifteen years. So they had to order it and it took twenty-four hours for the hospital to get the bed. I was literally just laying on a normal bed the first night before the RotoProne got delivered on Monday.

On Monday, they put me in that RotoProne bed for three weeks and it spins you like a rotisserie chicken over fire. It just kind of rotates you. The whole purpose of that was the pneumonia caused severe fluid in my lungs and that's what was limiting the amount of oxygen going to my brain. So they had to rotate my body so the fluids could splash around, if you will. And then, that allows air pockets to get through your lungs and to your brain to breathe. I survived the first seven days, but the doctors had no clue.

Well, I will say this—by the third day of being in the hospital, I hadn't been pronounced dead. It was either day two or day three, they never pronounced me dead. But they said that my body was crashing. My entire insides were completely shut down and they had to quote, unquote, "Bring me back." I was never pronounced dead, but they had to bring me back and get me stable and they had a machine pumping my heart.

And I was just a vegetable laying there because my SO2 levels, which normally are at 100%. The doctors want you at 97 or above, and that's a little scary because I was at 47%. Also, they didn't know if I had any brain activity. And they said anything under 50%, you're dead or you're in a retardation state. I hate that, using that word, but that's what they use where you're just a vegetable laying there.

And they did not know my brain activity until two weeks into my hospital stay. After the first two weeks, a nurse noticed my first brain activity. She told me personally that she cried and literally ran up and down the ICU hallways because they knew that there's sign of life.

So there is no sign of life in the first two weeks, and then, once two weeks hit, it is when I showed my first sign of life. I ended up having nineteen lines and tubes through me. I had multiple surgeries, blood clots, a trach. I have a fat scar on my neck and scars all over my body from surgeries that I was in. And after three weeks, I woke up . . . twenty-one days in the coma, I woke up.

And because this bed—it looks like something out of NASA—because this bed is so massive, they had to put me in the biggest room in the entire hospital. It was in a corner because your typical ICU room cannot handle this size bed. And so it was nice having a big room. So I remember, I woke up twenty-one days later and I opened up my eyes, and the first thing I see in front of me is a flat-screen TV. And three weeks prior, the last words that I heard was, "You're going to be dead in three hours. You have three hours to live." So in my mind, when I woke up, my first memory was looking at a TV. And, in my mind, I said, "Holy crap. There's TVs in heaven." Before I got sick, I was completely ripped and yoked, and

I had huge arms. So I look to my right and I see my arms were just scrawny, like tiny. I lost all my muscle. In the thirty days that I was in the hospital, I lost forty-two pounds and went from 210 to 168 pounds. And that's when I noticed all the lines in my body, and I ended up having nineteen lines and tubes going through me.

And then, using the energy that I had, I looked to my left and my mom is sitting there about two feet away, because she was by my bedside pretty much twenty-four seven. There are two times that she left the hospital to go shower and to get clean clothes. But other than, she was by my side twenty-four seven. And in my mind, I saw my mom and I thought, "Holy crap! Mom died and went to heaven too." And she was sitting with her legs crossed, and she pulled down her glasses. She was reading a magazine. She said, "Hey, honey!" And I couldn't speak so I was very, very confused. And that was that. My diagnosis, like I said, swine flu, which was H1N1, which was the pandemic that was ten-plus years ago. And 70 percent pneumonia on my lungs. And I had SARS, a severe acute respiratory syndrome. I was on twenty-four-hour dialysis. I mean, at age twenty-four, no one should be on full dialysis. So, like I said, my body crashed and that was that. So, I woke up and I could not sleep. I did not want to sleep.

I was in a coma for twenty-one days. Me and my girlfriend at the time had tickets to the Padres game. We had birthday parties. We had things scheduled. And when you're asleep for three weeks, it feels like you're asleep for one night. So I would say,

"Oh my gosh, we have Nicole's party." "Oh that was two weeks ago."

"Did he sell the Padres tickets?" "Oh that was three weeks ago." So it was really hard to comprehend that I'd been asleep for three weeks and not one day. With that being said, I felt mentally that if I were to fall asleep, I wouldn't wake up. So I was awake for three days straight. Seventy-two hours straight laying in a hospital bed with zero strength whatsoever. And I would just watch the clock pass. And again, I can't talk, I couldn't write, I had a feeding tube. I couldn't eat normal food. I just laid there helpless. And it was the second or third night of being awake and it was about 3:00 or 3:30 in the morning. I remember specifically it was either 3 or 3:30 and I still couldn't talk. And my parents brought in a CD player because that's what we used ten years ago. And they played Christian worship music to kind of set the tone in the room. And who they played, Casting Crowns, it's still to this day my all-time favorite Christian artist. And my favorite CD by them was the first CD they ever made.

Just so people know how sick I was, kind of backtracking. In the ICU, it's normally one nurse for every two patients. I had two nurses on me twenty-four seven because I was so critical. And the hospital, on the day that I got released on August 26 or August 24, told me that I was the sickest patient they'd ever had that left the hospital alive. So that's how critical I was.

So I buzzed the nurse. Her and I had this weird relationship that I would use my hands and she knew what I was trying to say. Like it was a godsend. I pointed to the music and I don't know what hand signals I used, but she got the hint. So she played the CD and she left, and it was just me in the room. And like I said, it was around 3:00 or 3:30 in the morning and I looked up into the pitch-black ceiling and I said, "Jesus let's talk." And I never died; my body never left the room. But I was instantly in heaven.

And I found myself swinging and in heaven with Jesus. I was on a swing to the left and he was on the right. I do not remember what I was wearing because looking back, that wasn't important at the time. I do remember that we were swinging. And we were sitting on wooden swings. And I would say the swing was like, I don't know, two feet long. Maybe like an old-school swing set. And I remember looking up and the swing ropes went into the sky. And there's a rope on each side of the swing that were tied in knots at the bottom. From there, the ropes went up into the clouds. And I remember, I never saw Jesus's face because he was just glowing. But he was in his white robe that the Bible describes. And we're swinging. I never saw streets of gold, but I did see the most beautiful green, grassy hills that anyone has ever seen. I mean, it made Petco Park or any NFL stadium or any MLB stadium on opening day look ugly. There was the most beautiful green grass, rolling hills, and we are swinging over heaven.

And as we're swinging, throughout the green rolling hills, as I wrote in my book, I describe it as about four feet of white pure concrete. And the concrete was like a beautiful concrete. I know that it sounds really weird, but that was the description of how pure heaven was and it was a concrete path that went throughout the rolling hills. And on this path were little kids full of joy and smiles, riding bikes.

About the CD that my parents played for me, Casting Crowns—their original album. I had grown to love the album when I went to Japan in 2005. I had the opportunity of going to Japan on a mission trip with my college for ten or twelve days and I fell in love with the CD. There were three songs I remember. The very first song is called "What If His People Prayed?" And then one of the songs is called "The Voice of Truth." Then, there's a third song that I can't remember the name of right now, but it's in my book. And the reason why this is important is because when I said, "Jesus, let's talk," and when I was ushered into heaven, the first song on the CD, "What If His People Prayed?" played throughout heaven. And it was like a battle cry loudspeaker. And as Jesus and I are swinging through heaven, I leaned over to him and I said, "Why are you doing this to me? You know, why me?"

And we had a conversation back and forth as we're swinging, and he just said, "You know, there are things that I need you to tell people when you get out of the hospital. There are things that I need you to bring back." And Second Chronicles 7:14 was brought up, which basically talks about men of God need to get on their knees and take a stand, and dust off their swords and actually pray, and God will heal the land. And the conversation was basically, you know, we need to do a better job of praying. If you're a believer, you got to pray, and so we talked about that. We had that conversation and we're swinging, swinging, swinging. The next song on the CD is called "The Voice of Truth" and again, it was like being blasted through the loudspeakers of heaven and these kids are just riding their bikes. When I say kids, I never saw teenagers, it's all like little kids. Like four-, five-, six-, seven-, eight-year-olds with smiles. Someone asked whether they were clothed or naked. It didn't matter at the time. I don't remember, but they're just having the time of their lives and we're swinging through heaven. And the song's called "The Voice of Truth," and it talks about how there's so many voices out there, you know, on a daily basis, but the true voice is the voice of God. And how Jesus was saying, you know, you need to tell people that I'm the one and the only true voice.

And then we're swinging and we went over hell. And when people think of hell, they think of fire and danger and heat. I never experienced that and never saw fire—never saw anything like that. What I did see was it was completely black. All black. And there was, I don't know, Adam, ten, fifteen, twenty feet of an open circle, of a pit, and it was I'd say between ten to twenty feet in circumference. I should say round. And there was a chain-linked fence. The sense (I had senses in heaven) was evil and disgusting and dirty, and I could smell the evil. I could feel the evil. I never saw flames or anything, but there were beasts. The closest that I can describe these freaks of nature was what looks like monkeys now. Some of them had like, I don't know, four, six, or eight arms. Some of them had two heads. And they were growling, they were screeching, and they were trying to grab me.

And again, I can't really describe or tell you what they were called, but they were as close to monkeys as I can describe, and there's several of them. And the thing that was important was, they were reaching for me, but they were on a chain. So they were chained. It wasn't a leash. It was like they were actual hard metal chains that clumped together and made noise, and even the chains were creepy. And I remember specifically what these things look like, and I remember some of them had like slime dripping off their bodies and they were just evil, evil, evil.

And I remember, as we were flying over the hole, one of them reached up to grab me and I reached over and grabbed on to Jesus's swing and he looked at me and said,

"What are you doing?"

And I said, "They're trying to get me." And I remember Jesus looking at me right in my eyes, and he said,

"They have no power over you. You're with me."

And I went back to my swing, and next thing I know, we're back over the green, wavy hills. Now, another song is being played, and I cannot remember the name of the song right now. But again, "What If His People Prayed" talks about prayer, the voice of truth, talking about hearing God's voice. And then the third one, I can't remember at this very moment, but Jesus and I would discuss that song. And next thing I knew, I was back in my hospital bed. It could have been three minutes in heaven. It could have been fifteen minutes in heaven. It could have been four hours in heaven. I don't believe that heaven has any time. We label time.

And the next day, I was crying all day because it was, you know—this experience was physical. It was emotional. And now it turned extremely spiritual, with having this heavenly out-of-body experience. And I cried literally the entire day. And the next day, they put what's called a Passy-Muir valve in my neck. A Passy-Muir valve is a little valve that goes into your tracheostomy—it's this little valve, you shove it through your neck and it allows you to talk. So I was able to speak, and I have this big clunky pipe coming out of my neck. My pastor at the time came down to visit me and I told him the story. Then, I said,

"People aren't going to believe me."

And he said, "There are going to be people who doubt. But God gave you that experience and you need to share it. Who cares what people think?" So that's why I wrote *Three Hours to Live*. And regarding the heavenly experience—I have spoken all over the place in the last ten years, and I always share my Jesus story. Let me tell you about three people I met that helped validate my experience. The first one: I shared my experience at the youth group that I was a youth pastor of when I got healthy enough to go back. This girl came up to me, and she said,

"My mom's picking me up from youth group tonight. I need you to talk to my mom." I said, "Okay." I had no idea what it's about. They were from Iran in the Middle East and this girl's mom and her dad had gotten in a really, really bad car accident in Iran, about three years prior to them moving to the United States. Her dad died on impact, and her mom was in a coma for three months. And in her coma, she had a heavenly experience with Jesus and she said that all she could describe was how beautiful the green hills of heaven were. So that was confirmation.

I spoke at a church in Poway, California. I was in a wheelchair at the time. And this woman, she was bucked off a horse, hit her head, and was in a semi-retardation state. And afterwards, when I was done speaking, her mom pushed her wheelchair up to me and said,

"I need you . . ." and she had tears in her eyes. And she said, "I need you to tell me the story again about heaven."

And I told her the heaven story and she started crying again.

And she said, "My daughter was bucked off a horse and she's now in a wheelchair, and she was right there and she said she was in a coma and when she woke up from her coma all she could talk about was how she was playing with Jesus on the most green, beautiful rolling hills in heaven."

And then the third one: I spoke at a church in Carlsbad, and this girl's nephew had just passed away. Just passed away like a week or two prior to me speaking. He lived in Texas and he had pneumonia. He was two years old, had pneumonia, and her dad called this girl to tell her that her nephew had just died. And her dad got a vision on the phone and said,

"Hey, you know, my little grandson just went to heaven and God put in my heart a vision of him running and playing in heaven's most beautiful, luscious green grass hills." So that was three confirmations about being able to be open about my story and knowing that people have experienced the same, because, when we think of heaven, we think of golden streets, right?

Regarding the evil monkey, what I call the evil monkey—I had to get counseling because I was very messed up in the head. You know, once I got out of the coma—the fourteen months of recovery were hell. And one of the counselors, I told him the evil monkey story, and he said when he was twenty-two years old, he had a fever of 105 degrees, and he thought he was going to die. And he went to the ER and they got him naked, completely naked, and they put him on his back on ice. And he said he was choking. And he opened his eyes, and he said there was an evil—what he could only describe as an evil monkey, straight from hell, that was choking the life out of him. And that was confirmation of these pure evil beasts, that these beasts are literally from hell and just plain evil. So that was confirmation there. The reason why I bring up the monkeys is because, when I woke up or when I came back from heaven and I woke up alone in the ICU room again, I couldn't move and I had a monitor that was feeding my, my . . . I had two feeding tubes through my nose and the monitor is about three feet over my head and it was the night after my heavenly experience. And I look up and that monkey was on my monitor in the ICU room in the hospital.

And I could see him. He was right above my head, and he was doing this thing with his hands. Like curling his hands and rubbing his chin, and it was pure evil. And making these gnawing sounds. And I couldn't do anything about it. And he was just hanging out right above me, three feet above my head. And everything about him was evil and I remember, I literally said the word "Jesus" a billion times this night. I just said over in my mind "Jesus Jesus Jesus Jesus Jesus," and I watched the sunrise because I fell asleep that night. And when the sun came up, he was gone. And that day, one of our good family friends came and put Bible verses up in the hospital room and prayed over every inch of the hospital room. And after they prayed, it was complete peace in the ICU.

Again, I was in recovery for fourteen months—to learn how to write, walk, spell, and everything. And to this day, my lungs are still completely jacked up. I get tired walking up a flight of stairs, but I make the most of it. And now I go around, and I'm able to share a story of how God saved me and how prayers work. And that's my story.

After we completed recording Jonny's NDE account, he asked if he could share another related experience that he hasn't spoken about often.

PART II

Okay, so going back really, really quick to the heaven thing. So the third song, I don't know if it matters. The third song is called, "If We Are the Body," and basically again, it was a song that was played all throughout heaven. And Jesus was telling me to bring back a message to the people. If we are the body, like if we are the body of Christ—an extension of Christ—then we need to be helping people out. The people that need it. And if we have money, we need to be helping people out there. Or if we have a gift or talent, we need to be helping people out as an extension of Christ. So those are the three songs.

So, I don't remember at what part of the coma this happened. It wasn't after the coma, when I had the heavenly experience with Jesus. I was awake for it. However, this experience that I'm about to share really quickly happened when I was in the coma. I don't know if it was a dream. I don't know if I physically went there. I don't remember, but it's probably the creepiest thing I've ever in my life experienced and it's gonna sound like a far-out nightmare. But I want to share it because this all happened on my near-death bed.

So, I was with my family. All six of us. I'm a very visual person and I'm very detailed when I try to tell a story, and I've only shared this with Lindsey (my wife) and my family, but not many other people, because it's such a trippy story. We were in a quote, unquote "Carnival," if you will, but it wasn't a carnival like you would think.

We were on the road, like a residential road. And there was a slight hill. And I remember specifically, we're walking up the hill and on the left side, on the corner, was this big, like, indoor stadium. But, not like the size of a baseball stadium. Like a movie theater, if you will, with stadium seating. And I don't know why I always remember this, but right outside, there's about eight to ten gray Porta Potties lining the outside. And I go in, and it was just me. I left my family; they were at the carnival.

And it was the weirdest thing. Imagine a massive movie theater with, I don't know, a couple hundred rows of seats that go up to the top back of the theater. So like stadium seating if you will. And where you'd walk up, where you would walk up, like in a movie theater, you'd walk up holding onto the rails. And how do I explain this? So there's normal seats. But, to walk up to get to the seats, and there's several hundred rows, it would kind of be like a roller coaster if you will. Well, like it was moving. I'm going to try to explain as best I can. It was continually moving. And it made like a "click, click, click, click, click" sound, and it was a track, if you will. But there is water on this track. So I walk in and I instantly get on the track and I noticed in front of me, to the left, hundreds of rows. And there's people. It isn't packed, but it was plenty full, and there's people. People in their seats. And I get on it on the track and there's water coming down.

And I go up, I go up, I go up, and then, when I get to the top, it kind of turns and then you go down on the other side. And you can get off the track any time and you can go sit if you want to. But then you go down. And once you go down to the bottom, it was a massive pool, a huge pool. So, just like a movie theater, there are the screens in front of you. There's a stage. But, instead of seats, there's a big pool. And, then you swim in the pool, and we had like, I remember a black, like, circular donut. People would just float in it. And then you go back on the track and you go up, you go up and then you go around, and you go back down and then you go back into the pool.

And I remember the two craziest things. There's a big fat stage, and it wasn't Satan but it was pure evil. And on the stage, was what looked like a dude. It looked look like a man. But the word that always came to my mind was "queen." It was like a queen and he or she, whatever it was, he or she was on the stage in this like king- or queen-size throne, if you will.

And I remember the throne chair was massive. And it sounded like he or she had a microphone, because the voice was so loud. The voice was so loud and it like, it was like it was a ruler. And this person again, wasn't Satan, but it was close to it. And this person was just absolute evil. And I remember the evil, evil laugh. I can't describe the music that was going on. Like the track was kind of like an amusement ride. Like an amusement park. Like when clowns come out. It's so hard to explain the music.

It's impossible to talk about the music that was playing through the loudspeaker. But it seems there's been two or three instances in the last ten years, where I'll hear a song, like at an amusement park or an entertainment center, and it instantly takes me back to this place. And the reason why this story is so important, why I don't like sharing it often, but I want to revisit it in the regression, is because I still don't know why I was there.

So we had the evil king or queen. Just pure evil. And the thing that I remember the most, which is so freaking odd, is when you went up onto the track, and you went around towards the back of the theater, and then you went back down and you went into the pool. Again, there's a big pool people could hang out in if they wanted to. There was little, I don't know if you remember, Adam, when we were younger you could go to Pizza Hut or the grocery store. You'd put a quarter in those little machines, little gumball machines, and sometimes there'd be a little bouncy ball. Sometimes there'd be like a little ring or something. And it was in those little plastic things. It was like a dome circle. And then it like clipped on underneath and those little things were impossible to get open. There were millions. Maybe not millions, but thousands of those floating in the pool in front of the evil queen.

But instead of toys, and this is why I don't remember why I was there but I want to know, instead of toys—so, imagine a pool completely full of these things floating, and instead of toys inside, there was a needle right in the center. So when you opened it up and took the lid off, there was a needle inside. I don't know, an inch and a half, two inches long. And the queen was forcing us to shove the needles in our mouth. And the needle went through the roof of our mouth. And every time that we had to go into the pool, we had to take a needle and shove it through our mouth. And that's probably one of the most vivid, gross visions and dreams or experiences I've ever had in my life. And the only thing I can say is it was an evil queen, like a demon. A demon queen. And I remember them forcing those needles through the top, through the roof of our mouth.

And again, the music. (Silence) Just the music was this evil, creepy, creepy music. And two or three times in the past ten years, I've heard the music in real life, and it now triggers me instantly back to that experience.

After we concluded recording Jonny's NDE account, he and I explored questions and open areas that we would explore during his regression.

- Why did you save my life, but not Ryan's or Rory's?

    Note: Ryan and Rory were two of Jonny's friends who passed away early in life. Jonny wanted to know why he was allowed to live and his friends were taken.

- What's my purpose in life?
- Why did Jesus pick me?
- Why did my mom pass on so early in life?

    Note: Jonny's mom, Teresa, crossed over two weeks before we recorded Jonny's NDE story.

- Why is there so much pain and heartache in my life?
- What was that movie theater–like place I went to with the pool? Who was the evil queen?

In our regression session, I took Jonny into a hypnotic state and then set the intention for him to experience whatever serves his soul's greatest good as it related to his NDE. The following is a transcript of Jonny's regression session.

Jonny's NDE Regression

Like Judy, I facilitated Jonny's NDE regression a week after he shared the account of his near-death experience. Jonny arrived to the Zoom session ready to revisit his NDE and get the closure he requested during his intake. I spent ten minutes getting Jonny into a deeply relaxed hypnotic trance. Once Jonny was induced into a hypnotic trance, I asked him to use his powerful imagination to visualize a hallway with many doors, with each of the doors representing an experience or a set of memories from his life. I then asked Jonny to find a door that seemed to stand out from the others and walk up to it. Once Jonny arrived at the door, he let me know by saying, "I'm here." Then, I connected Jonny with the intention that we set for the regression and asked him to walk through the door. The below is a verbatim transcription of Jonny's regression session.

* Jonny walks through the door—
Adam:
Jonny, tell me what you see.

Jonny:
I'm back in the swings in heaven right now, floating, and I see the hills and the grass, kids riding bikes. I'm back to heaven.

Adam:
That's awesome.

Jonny:
My legs are kicking in the air and we're going quite fast, faster than I remember. I can hear the sound of children playing and smiling. I can feel peace and freedom. I can see white clouds against perfect blue sky, like baby blue sky. My arms are holding onto the ropes.

Adam:
Are you with anyone?

Jonny:
I don't know yet. All I can see is the kids below me.

Adam:
Do you have any idea who those kids are?

Jonny:
I have no idea who they are.

Adam:
Okay.

Jonny:
I see Jesus to my right.

Adam:
Is he on the right-hand side of the swing and you're on the left or—?

Jonny:
He's on my right-hand side on His own swing, just like when I went to heaven.

Adam:
Oh, okay. Got it. So you're on two different swings and he's on the—

Jonny:
We're on two different swings.

Adam:
Okay.

Jonny:
He's on my right side and I'm to his left. We're kicking our legs in the swings, like on the schoolyard playground.

Adam:
That's awesome. That's awesome. So how does it feel? How are you feeling right now?

Jonny:
Complete and pure peace, no worries, no stress, full of joy. I feel like I don't weigh anything. I feel like I'm just free right now.

Adam:
Enjoy that for a minute.

Jonny:
Peaceful. (Silence)

Adam:
Yeah. Just let that sink in. I know you had some questions, Jonny. With Jesus sitting there next to you, this is a great opportunity to get some details and see if you can get answers. The first question, Jonny, that you wanted to review with Jesus was, why did you save my life but not Ryan's or Rory's? Did you want to ask Jesus that?

Jonny:
Should I ask him out loud or should I ask him in my mind?

Adam:
Ask him out loud or in your mind, either way, but let me know what he says in his response.

Jonny:
Just that it was their time and not mine. That's all that I need to know and to trust him.

Adam:
Okay. Excellent. Excellent. Another question you had, Jonny, was what is your purpose in life?

Jonny:
To reach millions of people, to serve people, to show people Jesus.

Adam:
Good.

Jonny:
To raise the family that he gave me.

Adam:
So, Jonny, you also wanted to know why Jesus picked you.

Jonny:
He wasn't expecting this one. What I'm getting is that people will listen to me, that I have influence over people. Part of that was through the book I wrote. A lot of answers are in the book, the book that I wrote.

Adam:
Yeah. That's awesome.

Jonny:
Because he told me to write, to come back and tell people, and I told people through my story.

Adam:
It's okay. Just keep with it, Jonny. Just stay with it where you are. You're doing great.

Jonny:
Yeah. I'm getting influence. I'm getting the word "influence" right now.

Adam:
Okay, good.

Jonny:
Not popuiarity, but influence. That there's a respect there that people will listen to.

Adam:
Yeah. That's awesome. That's awesome. Jonny, are you ready to dig into maybe a couple of more difficult questions for Jesus?

Jonny:
Yes.

Adam:
Okay. So Jon, I know one of the questions you had was, why is there so much pain and heartache in your life?

Jonny:
Yes. That was quick. Jesus just spoke to me and said there's a verse in the Bible that says, "In this life you will have trouble. But take hold, I have overcome the world. In this life you will have trouble. But hold on, I have overcome the world." That's all I need to know right now.

Adam:
Okay. Awesome. Awesome.

Jonny:
I'm getting trust and faith.

Adam:
Yeah.

Jonny:
Trust and faith, and that some things will be revealed down the road.

Adam:
That's awesome. All right, Jon. Go ahead.

Jonny:
I'm getting a vision of a racehorse running down the track and there's blinders on the racehorse. But as the horse is running and I'm the horse, as I'm going full speed ahead the blinders are slowly coming off. That's the vision that I'm getting right now. I have to run full speed ahead in trust, and as I obey and trust with faith, God's going to remove the blinders as I continue to run the race. It's not for me to see yet, but it will be revealed to me down the road. It's a racehorse, but it's not an oval track.

The track is just straight and it doesn't end. It's just straight. The message I'm getting is to run the race and don't give up. Even when life gets tough, you got to keep running the race.

Adam:
Jon, do you want to ask Jesus about why your mom passed on so early in life?

Jonny:
Yes, I do. All I'm getting is that he needed her. He needed her and . . . hold on. And it's on us to carry out the legacy that she's leaving behind. That's all I'm getting on that.

Adam:
Okay. This wasn't one of your questions, but do you . . . This is up to you. If you want to ask this, you can. If not, just say, "Let's move on to the next thing." But if you feel like you want to, ask Jesus if he can bring your mother forward one more time, go ahead and do that.

Jonny:
Yeah, I'm okay with that.

Adam:
Okay. Just let him know you'd like to see her again.

> Note: In certain types of hypnotic regressions, it is possible to bring those who have crossed over into the experience.

Jonny:
I don't see a body, but I see her smiling face. It's before she got sick. I don't know if it's my imagination. I don't know if it's a photographic memory, but it's her beautiful face, sitting at a table with that gap between her teeth and the sunshine or, I don't know. It could be her sitting at a table at the park or it could be her sitting at a table in heaven, because I see the beautiful grass behind her. She's at peace and she's got a big smile.

Adam:
Is there anything you want to say to her now that you can see her and she can communicate back?

Jonny:
Just how much I love her and how much I miss her.

Adam:
Yeah. You can say that to her directly.

Jonny:
I love you and I miss you, Mom. I don't know if she can see me or hear me—

Adam:
She can.

Jonny:
. . . But I can see her.

Adam:
She can. She's hearing everything you're saying right now.

Jonny:
I miss you, Mom. We love you. The girls talked about you today, Mom. Not a minute goes by that we don't not miss you. We're carrying out your legacy every single day. I think what I'm seeing is I'm seeing her in heaven. My body is so light right now. It's like it's floating. It's weird. It's so weird.

Adam:
It's awesome.

Jonny:
I feel like I'm on a waterbed of clouds.

Adam:
Well, that's because you've been there before and you know where you are. You're home.

Jonny:
It's so nice.

Adam:
Is Jesus still with you?

Jonny:
Let me look. I'm going to get back into that place of heaven.

Adam:
Okay.

Jonny:
Yeah, we're there. We're back.

Adam:
Okay. I know there was an area, Jon, that you explored. I believe it was while you were on the swing. Correct me if I'm wrong here, but when you were flying over heaven and then you saw this darkness. You flew over this darkness and there was a pool that . . . Am I remembering that correctly?

Jonny:
Hell?

Adam:
Yeah. There was a woman.

Jonny:
Oh, oh, oh. No. We flew over hell and heaven; the woman queen was
during a dream.

Adam:
Okay. Okay. Did you want to explore either the hell or the
dream experience?

Jonny:
We can explore both.

Adam:
Okay. Okay. Why don't you ask Jesus if he'll accompany you over to what
you experienced as hell?

Jonny:
Okay. It got dark.

Adam:
What are you seeing? What's around you?

Jonny:
I'm back there right now. It's not a good place. It's confusion—

Adam:
Is Jesus with you?

Jonny:
Yeah, He's to my right.

Adam:
Okay, good.

Jonny:
It's confusion and chaos.

Adam:
What is—

Jonny:
I can smell the evil and I can hear the evil.

Adam:
Do you want to ask Jesus where you are, what that is?

Jonny:
I can see the pit, that chain-link fence and the evil, the evil creatures. But
I already know that there's no power over my life, so it doesn't scare me.
There's no need to grab onto his swing right now because I'm free.

Adam:
Did you want to know why you were shown that at all in your NDE?

Jonny:
I do want to know. I'm getting the download that he's putting it back on me. He said, "You already know." I already know the answer. It's because hell is just as real as heaven, and you spend eternity at one of those two places. I'm not afraid this time around though, like I was . . . (Silence)

Jonny:
. . . The first time.

Adam:
That's good. That's good. Is there anything else in hell, while you're there, that you . . . it sounds like a funny question, but that you want to explore?

Jonny:
No.

Adam:
Okay. Okay. What I want you to do, Jon, just keep Jesus close, and I want you, in your mind, to go back and revisit the nightmare you had. I want you to imagine or just think of that carnival music from the dream. Just allow that music to transport you to a place that's most relevant to that music and bring Jesus along with you as well.

Jonny:
Should I go inside the door to the arena?

Adam:
Yeah, absolutely. Go wherever you feel guided, Jon. This is your journey.

Jonny:
I'm inside.

Adam:
What do you see?

Jonny:
The same setup. The evil queen is on the stage and we're going up the edge on the track. That scary music's being played.

Adam:
How far away is she from you?

Jonny:
I'm all the way at the top at the very back of the arena.

Adam:
Okay.

Jonny:
And she's on the stage. The water's trickling down and now I'm going to go down the right side of the track into the big pool.

Adam:
Is there any way you can get close enough to her where she can hear you?

Jonny:
I'm heading down right now.

Adam:
Okay. Let me know when you get to a place where she's close enough to hear you.

Jonny:
Those little plastic things with the needles are all over the pool, all over the water. I'm in front of the evilness, the Satanic queen.

Adam:
Why don't you ask her who she is?

Jonny:
A worker of Satan. I don't know where that came from because she didn't say anything. But that's what I'm getting.

Adam:
Okay. She could be communicating telepathically. What is she doing? What is this place? Where are you?

Jonny:
I don't understand that.

Adam:
You don't understand what she's saying to you?

Jonny:
Yeah. It's like a screeching and hollering and evil, evil.

Adam:
Can you ask Jesus where you are, where the place is?

Jonny:
No answer.

Adam:
Okay.

Jonny:
I'm not getting anything there.

Adam:
Okay. That's fair.

Jonny:
But I'm back at that place. I don't see Jesus here inside.

Adam:
What place?

Jonny:
I'm at the arena with the carnival music.

Adam:
Oh, so Jesus didn't go in with you.

Jonny:
But I can feel his presence though.

Adam:
Okay.

Jonny:
So I'm not afraid of the needles and I'm not afraid of the evil queen. The music isn't doing anything to me in a bad way.

Adam:
Okay. This is different than before, because you had a fear of that, right?

Jonny:
100 percent.

Adam:
Why don't you tell her that she has no more control or power over you?

Jonny:
You have no power or control over my thoughts or over me, none. She's just sitting on this chair with this proud glare, evil glare with this big rod-looking stick, just evil. She's big too. It's not your normal, average female. It's a large person, not large as in fat, just a big, tall, evil queen.

> Note: One of the goals of hypnotherapy is to ensure clients received the closure needed in order to move forward in life. Jonny received closure with his rebuke of the evil queen.

Adam:
Is there anything else about that place you want to . . . *(Jonny interjects)*

Jonny:
I want to know where it is and I'm not getting that. I don't know if that's important right now or ever, because I've tried to figure it out and I've never figured it out why I was sent there or what the importance is.

Adam:
So can you walk outside? Do you still see the door where you walked in?

Jonny:
I'm right next to it.

Adam:
Okay. So go ahead and walk outside. What do you see around you?

Jonny:
I see a carnival, like a fair on a street.

Adam:
Is there anybody there?

Jonny:
Just random people walking.

Adam:
Can you stop one of them and ask them where you are?

Jonny:
It doesn't make any sense to me because when I was there ten years ago and when I'm now here, in my mind right now, it's in Ramona. It's a street in the Country Estates. But it doesn't make any sense why the evil arena would be in the Country Estates.

Adam:
Yeah. No need to analyze it.

Jonny:
It's in Ramona. It's in the Country Estates by the Ramona Oaks Park.

Adam:
Okay. Interesting. Interesting. Okay. Anything else that you want to explore in this space?

Jonny:
No. There's families skipping up and down the road. There's stands of cotton candy and popcorn. I don't think anyone's aware of what's going on inside the arena.

Adam:

I was just going to ask you if you could stop someone and ask them if they knew what was going on in the arena. Is there—

Jonny:

I can't get anyone. It's as if they're just doing their own thing, drumming to their own beat and not stopping.

Adam:

Okay. Okay.

Jonny:

But my body right now at this moment feels completely, again, like I'm floating, completely lifeless. It's a weird, weird—like I weigh nothing right now. Maybe that's just because I'm so relaxed.

Adam:

Well, maybe you can float back up to where you were with Jesus on the swing and see if you can get Jesus back into your consciousness.

Jonny:

Let me get there.

Adam:

Okay.

Jonny:

I'm floating on the swing in heaven with Jesus again.

Adam:

Okay. If you want, you can ask Jesus if there's anything else he wants to say to you or anything he wants you to know before you head back.

Jonny:

I'm not getting anything currently.

Adam:

Okay. That's fine.

Jonny:

He's there. He's right next to me though.

Adam:

Then he just may not have anything more to say. The only other question I have for you, and again, this is personal. I just want to make sure that I bring it into your awareness, in case it's something you want to experience. So I know earlier we asked about Ryan and Rory. Would you like to call forward to their souls? If that's something you'd like to experience, you're more than welcome to do so now.

Jonny:
I would love to. (Silence)

Adam:
Okay. Are they coming through at all, Jonny?

Jonny:
They are. I'm talking to them.

Jonny:
I can see their whole bodies, their full bodies, their heavenly bodies, their goofy smiles. They're right in front of me, right next to me, a foot away.

Adam:
That's awesome.

Jonny:
Happy, healthy, giggly. Rory is very black and dark, and he's got a glow on him, like a heavenly glow, like an angel. He looks angelic. Ryan's just Ryan. He's just a goofball. I said I can't believe it's been ten years, and he had kind of a puzzled look like, "ten years?" We hold onto time, not them. They're just laughing. Both of them are laughing. Wow. This is wild. They say that they're fine and not to worry about them. It's like they just disappeared. Poof, and they were gone.

Adam:
All right, my friend. Is there anything else you wish to explore while you're in your realm?

Jonny:
It's so peaceful up here.

Adam:
Just take some time and enjoy the peace.

Jonny:
Yeah.

CHAPTER VI

JOLENE

I met Jolene at an intuitive event in the beginning of 2020, and we quickly become friends. When Jolene learned about the NDE research I was conducting, she asked if she could participate. You'll find that Jolene's NDE account is rather short and to the point. However, the regression we did together was a beautiful exploration and follow-up to her near-death experience.

Jolene's NDE Account

Jolene: Yeah, so I ended up having cancer at twenty-two and went through five years of surgery. And the last surgery, I was twenty-six years old. And I went into surgery and woke up with nurses and people attending to me yelling at me, things like, "You know, you're the oldest one in surgery this morning and you died on the table," and I remember very vividly going to the other side/home. And I was sitting on a bench talking to my grandmother who kept saying, "All of the questions you want answered are right through the doors." And, then we talked for a while longer, and then she'd repeat it again. And I'd had lots of questions. So then we talked a little bit more, and then she repeated it one more time, "All the questions you have are right through the doors." Well the minute I stood, I said, "Grandma, you know, it's been awesome talking to you, but I really need my questions answered." And the minute I stood up she's like, "I'm sorry, it's not your time. You have to go back. You still have a lot of things to complete." So that was pretty much the gist of that story. And, then in about 2005 or 2008, I was reading a book by Sylvia Browne who had pictures of her guide, which her guide had given her, of what it looked like on the other side. And when I looked at the pictures, they looked like exactly where I was sitting talking to my grandmother. It was called "The Hall of Wisdom." The Hall of Wisdom was full of beautifully architected columns and a large staircase. While Sylvia's depiction shows people in the Hall, I didn't see anyone else. It was just my grandmother and I sitting on a bench talking. So that's pretty much my story.

Adam: Jolene, when your grandma was telling you that all of the answers you need were through the doors, were you able to see what was behind the doors?

Jolene: The minute I stood up, she's like, "I'm sorry. It's not your time. You have to go back." Okay, I had two little boys that were like, two and four, so I had things to do here yet. It wasn't my time. So I was sent back.

Adam: And how long did it feel like you were out of body? Was it quick? Was it short?

Jolene: It actually felt like it was a long time because I mean we would talk and talk and talk and then, and then she would bring it up, "All your questions are right through the doors." And then we would talk and talk and talk, and, I don't know, it felt like half an hour to an hour. To me anyway.

Adam: And do you recall the conversations that you and your grandma were having?

Jolene: I don't. I don't. All I remember her saying over and over again is, "All the questions you have are right through the doors." And she knew where to get me because, you know, ever since I was very small, I've always had so many questions about things that just never got answered. Nobody could answer them.

I believe I have had a few NDEs. I went through a rough time at seventeen and tried to commit suicide, but I don't remember anything at all. I don't remember going anywhere or anything happening. I was also very sick for my kindergarten shots at age five; I kind of suspect I had a near-death experience, but nobody ever talked about it or told me about it. I just remember them. I remember going into the hospital with a really high fever. They threw me in tubs of ice and I went in and out of consciousness a lot.

Then, when I was three, my mom was very abusive and would lock me outside in the chicken coop at night. My dad was at work, and I think something might have happened there. But, I just don't know for sure and would like to find out.

After we wrapped recording Jolene's NDE account, she shared a few questions that she wanted to cover during her regression session.

- What was my grandmother telling me while we were talking?
- How many lifetimes has my soul lived and what is the average lifetimes for most people?
- In what year did I live my very first lifetime? And what year was I born?
- How many NDEs have I had in this lifetime?

- What is my connection with aliens and will they be taking me to their planet? If so, when?

  Note: Jolene says that she's had many communications with extraterrestrial beings

- What is my purpose on Earth this time?
- How old is my soul?

In our regression session, I took Jolene into a hypnotic state and then set the intention for her to experience whatever serves her soul's greatest good as it related to her NDE. The following is a transcript of Jolene's regression session.

Jolene's NDE Regression

I facilitated Jolene's NDE regression two weeks after she shared the account of her near-death experience. I was interested to see if Jolene's regression would be as brief as her NDE account. After getting Jolene into a deeply relaxed hypnotic trance, I asked her to use her powerful imagination to visualize a hallway with many doors, with each of the doors representing an experience or a set of memories from her life. I then asked Jolene to find a door that seemed to stand out from the others and walk up to it. Once Jolene arrived at the door, she let me know by saying, "I'm here." Then, I connected Jolene with the intention that we set for the regression and asked her to walk through the door. The below is a verbatim transcription of Jolene's regression session.

Jolene walks through the door—

Adam:
Jolene, tell me what you see.

Jolene:
I'm not seeing anything. It's like blue and black and stars.

Adam:
Okay. Good. Good. And do you get a feeling or a sense of the place that you're at? What does it feel like?

Jolene:
Just feels like I'm floating.

Adam:
Great.

Jolene:
Just light.

Adam:
Okay. Are you able to look down and see your feet? Can you tell if you're wearing anything on your feet?

Jolene:
No, I don't think I am.

Adam:
Okay. So you feel like you're barefoot? Is that what you're saying?

Jolene:
Yes. Yes, barefoot.

Adam:
Okay, great. And do you get a sense of what you look like? Are you seeing anything yet?

Jolene:
Not really. (Silence)

Adam:
Okay.

Jolene:
Strange. (Silence)

Adam:
If you look down, are you able to see what you're wearing?

Jolene:
I think it's a robe. (Silence)

Adam:
What does the robe look like?

Jolene:
It's long. Kind of a cream color. It's got a tie. (Silence)

Jolene:
Like a gold tie around the waist. Not a tie but a rope, cut more like a rope.

Adam:
Excellent.

Jolene:
It's comfortable.

Adam:
Good.

Jolene:
Comfortable.

Adam:
And as you look out, what do you see?

Jolene:
Not seeing anybody.

Adam:
It doesn't have to be anybody. Are you seeing— (Jolene interjects)

Jolene:
It's just a—Yeah, I just see columns and cement.

Jolene:
Staircase.

Adam:
Okay. Are you able to walk up to the staircase?

Jolene:
Yes.

Adam:
Okay. Can you describe what you're seeing when you look around?

Jolene:
Just looks pristine, clean. There's some trees, flowers. It's beautiful. There's a stream. I'm still not seeing any people.

Adam:
It's okay. What does it feel like? What are you feeling right now?

Jolene:
Just love and joy, happiness. Body just still feels super light. I'm not sure I'm even walking. Feels like you float, sort of above the ground level. (Silence)

Adam:
Now you may not see anybody, but do you get a sense if there are any other beings around?

Jolene:
Yes. I feel like there's people.

Adam:
Okay. Okay.

Jolene:
I don't know, I can feel just like love radiating from them.

Adam:
Great. Do you get a sense of whether it's anyone in particular? Or a group of people? Are you able to get that sense?

Jolene:
It just feels like we're all family.

Adam:
Okay.

Jolene:
Sort of we're just all connected. Feels like a big family.

Adam:
And do you see them? Or is it something you're sensing.

Jolene:
I just feel them.

Adam:
Okay. Good. You're doing great, Jolene.

Jolene:
It's beautiful. It's just beautiful. Feels like home.

Adam:
Good. Just take it in. Allow yourself to take all of it in. And when you're ready, Jolene, why don't you call out and ask if any of the beings or the energy that you're feeling will manifest itself and show itself to you.

Jolene:
"Show yourself to me." It's an alien.

Adam:
It's an alien?

Jolene:
Yeah. (Silence)

Adam:
Can you describe what the alien looks like?

Jolene:
Oh, it's like I'm only seeing from the shoulders up and the head. And it's really, it almost looks like just bone. Big eyes. A smaller nose, a smaller mouth. The eyes are really big. It knows I see him.

Adam:
Do you want to ask who this alien is?

Jolene:
Jolene asks, "Who are you?"

Jolene's shown: He's my father. He said call me father. (Silence) He's saying he's everybody's father. (Silence)

Adam:
What does that mean?

Jolene:
It means that he's everybody's father. Everybody that's there, he's . . . I get the impression and feel that he just, everybody looks up to him. He's not the father of everyone. But yet he said he is, but not physical. Someone very important.

Adam:
Can you ask him where you are right now? (Silence)

Jolene:
It feels like deep space.

Adam:
Okay.

Jolene:
I see a wormhole, traveling through wormholes to get there.

Adam:
And is this the place, Jolene, that you went to when you were talking with your grandmother in your NDE?

Jolene:
I don't think so.

Adam:
Okay. So this is a different place. Okay.

Jolene:
Yeah.

Adam:
Okay. So do you get a sense for this alien's name?

Jolene:
He just says Father.

Adam:
Okay.

Jolene:
As a name.

Adam:
Okay. Will you ask Father how many lifetimes you have lived? And then what the average number of incarnations are for most people? (Silence)

Jolene:
He's saying 780. The average is 800. (Silence)

Adam:
Can you ask him what the year was that you were born in for your very first incarnation? (Silence)

Jolene:
11.

Adam:
So the year 11.

Jolene:
Yes.

Adam:
Okay. And how—

Jolene:
BC.

Adam:
BC, okay.

Jolene:
BC.

Adam:
Okay. And is he able to give you a sense for how old your soul is? (Silence)

Jolene:
Just very old.

Adam:
Okay. Okay.

Jolene:
Much older. (Silence)

Adam:
Does he have anything that he wants to say to you? (Silence)

Jolene:
No.

Adam:
Does he know how many NDEs that you've had in this lifetime? (Silence)

Jolene:
Three.

Adam:
Three. Okay. (Silence) And is Father able to possibly bring forward the energy of your grandmother? (Silence)

Jolene:
He's saying she's not there.

Adam:
Okay. Can you ask where she is?

Jolene:
A different planet.

Adam:
What does that mean, Jolene? Does that mean that she reincarnated or she's, where her soul is, is a different planet?

Jolene:
She reincarnated.

Adam:
Okay. (Silence) You mentioned that you see wormholes around. Is that correct?

Jolene:
I did, yes.

Adam:
Okay. Are they not there anymore?

Jolene:
Not right now.

Adam:
Okay. Are you able to ask Father, since your grandmother isn't there, if he knows about the conversation that you were having with your grandmother when you experienced your near death? Is he able to fill you in?

Jolene:
Yes, some of it. She was telling me that I had to go back. My boys needed me. It wasn't my time. *(Silence)*

Adam:
Jolene, are you able to ask Father if he can take you back to the place you went, where the doors were? The doors in your NDE that you were not allowed to enter. Can you move there?

Jolene:
Yes.

Adam:
Okay. Let me know when you're there. *(Silence)*

Jolene:
All right. I'm going to the wormhole. *(Silence)*

Adam:
And have you gotten there yet?

Jolene:
Still seeing the wormhole.

Adam:
Okay. *(Silence) Just take your time.*

Jolene:
Is that what I'm supposed to see?

Adam:
The wormhole?

Jolene:
Yes.

Adam:
It might be. Are you alone or are you with somebody right now?

Jolene:
I feel alone.

Adam:
Okay.

Jolene:
But I feel a little tense, like somebody's here.

Adam:
Okay. And do you get a sense for who that is?

Jolene:
I'm not sure. I can't see them.

Adam:
Okay. Do you want to ask who's with you in the wormhole? Can you ask?

Jolene:
Who's with me? He won't say his name. He just seems creepy.

Adam:
Okay. So Jolene, what I want you to do is I want you to just move forward to the place where you and your grandma sat. You have the ability and the power to move right out of that wormhole to that building and the closed doors you experienced during your NDE. Let me know when you're there. (Silence)

Jolene:
Okay.

Adam:
Are you there now?

Jolene:
Yes.

Adam:
Okay. Can you describe what the place looks like where you're at?

Jolene:
It almost seems like a cave of some sort. But there's doors. It's almost like a cathedral dug out with the point on the top. Just seems to go on forever.

Adam:
And do the doors look at all like you remember it from your near-death experience?

Jolene:
Yeah.

Adam:
They do?

Jolene:
Yeah.

Adam:
Okay. Are you able to walk up to the doors?

Jolene:
Yes.

Adam:
Okay. Let me know when you're there.

Jolene:
I'm there, I'm there. I'm there.

Adam:
Okay. And is anybody else around?

Jolene:
I see a shadow of a child.

Jolene:
In the hall.

Adam:
Okay. Can you ask the shadow who it is?

Jolene:
He said he was my son. The one I lost.

Adam:
Okay. You're doing really well.

Jolene:
Yeah.

Adam:
And how does he feel?

Jolene:

He's happy.

Adam:
Okay.

Jolene:
Happy to see me. And he's happy there.

Adam:
Can you ask him if he's able to help you walk through the doors to get to the answers on the other side? The answers that you've been looking for.

Jolene:
Yeah. He can do that.

Adam:
He said he can?

Jolene:
Yes.

Adam:
Okay. All right. Why don't you two walk through the doors and let me know what you see once you walk through.

Jolene:
It's so weird. It's just the universe and stars. It's like the whole room is just filled. And now I feel like I'm going through another wormhole.

Adam:
Okay. And is your son still with you?

Jolene:
I don't think so.

Adam:
Okay. (Silence)

Jolene:
Something's blocking me.

Adam:
Something's blocking you?

Jolene:
Yes.

Adam:
Blocking you from where?

Jolene:
Nowhere. It feels like my mind.

Adam:
How do you mean?

Jolene:
I don't know.

Adam:
Is it that something's blocking you from the answers you're looking for?

Jolene:
That's how I feel, yes.

Adam:
Okay. Are you able to ask the energy or the entity, whoever's there, why they're blocking you from these answers? (Silence)

Jolene:
They don't want you to know.

Adam:
Who's they?

Jolene:
There's a group of people here now. Wormhole's full of people.

Adam:
Okay.

Jolene:
They're wearing long black robes. Heads are covered. I can see a few faces.

Adam:
Do you get a sense of who they are?

Jolene:
They feel like a council.

Adam:
Oh.

Jolene:
Council members.

Adam:
Okay. What is their role there?

Jolene:
"We are the council. We govern and rule over all who reside here." I'm feeling tense again.

Adam:
Okay.

Jolene:
He's pretty serious.

Adam:
Okay, good. Do you feel like, do they feel familiar? What is the feeling?

Jolene:
Yes, I've met them before. They kind of scare me a little.

Adam:
Can you ask them what's on the other side of the doors?

Jolene:
Everything. All the answers.

Adam:
Can you ask why you can't have the answers?

Jolene:
They don't want me to know all the answers.

Adam:
Okay. Is there anything they want you to know? Is there anything they want to share with you?

Jolene:
They said, "We'll be together soon." (Silence) Everything's going to be all right.

Adam:
Is there anything that they can tell you about your life or your purpose in this life while you're here?

Jolene:
Yes, purpose is to heal. Heal others. Spread joy and love. That's my purpose.

Adam:
Good.

Jolene:
Teach. Teach and heal. (Silence)

Adam:
Are they able to tell you what your relationship to the aliens were/are?

Jolene:
Yes, we are related. I'm a star seed. I've visited it before.

Adam:
You visited where before?

Jolene:
A whole planet.

Adam:
Okay.

Jolene:
It's beautiful.

Adam:
Are you seeing the planet now?

Jolene:
Yes. It has high glass towers, lush greenery, purple lighting. It's someone standing beside me. Seems like he's twelve feet tall. I feel very safe with him.

Adam:
Can you ask him who he is?

Jolene:
He's my husband.

Adam:
Your husband in another life?

Jolene:
Yes.

Adam:
Okay. (Silence) Is there anything that he wants to tell you about yourself or about your experience?

Jolene:
He wants me to come home to help him rule. (Silence)

Adam:
Can you ask him when that's going to, when you're going to be able to go back home? Is it after this life? Is it after another life? Does he know?

Jolene:
He's saying it will be during this life. (Silence) They want me to come for a visit.

Adam:
Can he tell you how you're going to transport there? How is that going to work?

Jolene:
They'll just pick me up.

Adam:
Okay.

Jolene:
I see some kind of a tube that they put me in. And they go through the wormholes at the speed of light, very fast. (Silence) They want me to be a spokesperson for them on this planet.

Adam:
On Earth?

Jolene:
Yes, on Earth. (Silence)

Adam:
Is there anything else they want you to know? Or he wants you to know?

Jolene:
All will be revealed. I already have the information through downloads. All will be revealed soon.

Adam:
Good. Jolene, are there any other questions you want to ask about your life or about anything? Really, this is your chance to get whatever answers that are still on your mind.

Jolene:
How long do I have left on this Earth? (Silence) About twelve years. It's hard to take. I don't think there's anything else.

Adam:
Okay.

Jolene:
That I can think of.

Jolene:
Oh, my God.

Adam:
What are you seeing?

Jolene:
I was just seeing a bunch of aliens. Different shaped faces, babies. Okay, I'm done.

Adam:
No, explore it. What are you . . .

Jolene:
They seem mad that I told you.

Adam:
Can you ask them why they're mad?

Jolene:
I'm not supposed to tell.

Adam:
Not supposed to tell what?

Jolene:
I'm not supposed to tell you. They don't want me to tell you.

Adam:
That you're seeing them?

Jolene:
Yes.

Adam:
And what's the risk of—

Jolene:
I see a bunch of women now with their hands over their mouths. I'd say there's sixty to a hundred.

Adam:
Are they human women or alien women?

Jolene:
They look like half and half. I mean like a combination of the two together. (Silence) Oh wow, there's a lot more. Rows and rows and rows.

Adam:
And who are they?

Jolene:
They're called half-breeds. Half and half. I almost feel like breeders.

Adam:
And how are you connected to them?

Jolene:
I'm not sure. I feel like I started it. Started the breeder program. Oh, my heart's pumping really fast right now.

Adam:
It's okay, just breathe.

Jolene:
They don't like me very much.

Adam:
Oh. Can you ask them why they don't like you?

Jolene:
All of it, it feels very militarized. Like they only have a certain area they're allowed to be in. Very confined. (Silence) Yeah. They're gone now.

Adam:
Okay. All right. And where are you right now?

Jolene:
I feel like I'm, well, I moved away from them. (Silence)

Adam:
Okay. So here's what we're going to do, Jolene. You've had quite the multidimensional experience today. Let's bring you out of hypnosis.

Jolene:
Yeah.

CHAPTER VII

NOELLE

I met Noelle through a social media community where people share their NDEs. Shortly after posting that I was looking for volunteers for this research, Noelle messaged me. Noelle lives in Singapore and has brilliant NDE regression. In chapter III, I explain what current and past life regressions are. In Noelle's regression, she was shown memories from her current life and past lives before connecting with the Source of all energy and love. As you read through the transcripts of Noelle's NDE account and regression, please keep in mind that English is her second language. I did my best to preserve her words verbatim.

Noelle's NDE Account

Noelle: Yeah, so my near-death experience actually occurred when I was eight years old. I had emergency surgery which was not planned. Yeah. So what happened was, when I was being pushed to the surgical room, the surgeons and nurses actually opened me up. They thought that it was appendicitis, like inflammation of the appendix, because I have very bad tummy ache. And then, when they open me up, they actually saw a giant tumor, which was like about seven centimeters and it was attached to my ovary.

So they need to quickly prepare more anesthetic for me too. Yeah, for to put me down under and that they had to quickly alert my mom that they found the tumor, which could potentially be cancerous, and then to, you know, to . . . for her advice on what to do. So then, for me, I had out-of-body experiences. I actually floated out of my body in the same surgical room. It was an aerial view. I was at a corner, and I was looking down at everyone I saw. One of the surgeons, one of the doctors and all these other nurses surrounding my body. I could see them operating on me and the conversations that they had. You know, and it was very muffled. I couldn't hear very clearly. I was confused because I didn't know what they were doing to me. I don't know what such a surgery is at age of eight, but I saw them doing that to my body. But the feeling I had was—like it was very peaceful. It was like watching a movie clip. You know, I was very detached from everything. I was feeling very calm. There was no fear. There was no pain. I don't have any wants.

So, for example, I don't want to go back to my body, and I was just in a place where I'm looking down at what these people were doing. And I was really very objective and very peaceful. And now what happened after that was that I thought that I was violently being pulled back to my body, and then I woke up. I can remember the feeling that I had when I woke up. I was feeling very agitated. I was very angry. I was feeling, "Why was this happening to me?" You know, like, "Why do I have to go through this whole chaos? Why is this surgery happening?" And then it was a very, very violent action, like a cough. Like I was like crying, coughing, and I was being pulled back to my body. So that was my experience.

Adam: And do you remember when you had this experience, were you able to say anything to the doctors? Like, "Hey I saw you while I was outside of my body and I saw you doing one thing or another!" And, if so, did they validate anything that you saw? Or was there no conversation?

Noelle: There was no conversation because I was too young. But I knew that actually my blood pressure dropped to very low. It dropped to very low during the surgery and my mom was telling me they taught that I won't be able to survive it. Yeah, they don't tell me a lot of things because I was so young.

Also, before we end. I know I'm just different since I'm born. A lot of mystical, divine, and strange experiences, especially during childhood. For instance, able to recall being a fly in one of my past life, living from the perspective from it and then died. Seeing deities and hearing movement of spirits. Throughout the years, I realized that I have very high intuition and was able to sense people's feelings and thoughts. I didn't quite know what that was and why I took their feelings/wants as my own. Over this life, there seems to be some force/energy which wants to reveal realizations (truth?) to me, but I kept running away from it as otherwise I couldn't lead a normal life (e.g., set up a family/hold down a job/ operate in a normal way).

And just last year, I found out that I had a genetic disease. I have a problem at a DNA level. Which made my body physically different from "normal." So I wanted to know, why am I different?

After we wrapped recording Noelle's NDE account, she shared a few questions that she wanted to cover during her regression session.

- Why am I still here? Why did I come back into my body?
- How can I heal from what I'm going through now?
- Why do I experience so many ups and downs, pain and suffering in this life?
- I found out that I had a genetic disease. I have a problem at a DNA level. Which made my body physically different from "normal." So I want to know, why am I different?
- How is my son related to me? I know we have a really deep connection.
- Why do I keep seeing the numbers 1111? What is the message?

In our regression session, I took Noelle into a hypnotic state and then set the intention for her to experience whatever serves her soul's greatest good as it related to her NDE. The following is a transcript of Noelle's regression session.

Noelle's NDE Regression

After getting Noelle into a deeply relaxed hypnotic trance, I asked her to use her powerful imagination to visualize a hallway with many doors, with each of the doors representing an experience or a set of memories from her life. I then asked Noelle to find a door that seemed to stand out from the others and walk up to it. Once Noelle arrived at the door, she let me know by saying, "I'm here." Then, I connected Noelle with the intention that we set for the regression and asked her to walk through the door. The below is a verbatim transcription of Noelle's regression session.

Noelle walks through the door—

Adam:
Okay, Noelle. What do you see?

> *Note: At this point, Noelle is being shown childhood memories from her current life.*

Noelle:
I'm drowning. I'm drowning.

Adam:
You're drowning?

Noelle:
Yeah.

Adam:
Okay.

Noelle:
I can feel vibration throughout my body, vibration is the waves. Come help me.

Adam:
Okay, and are you in . . . Can you describe the place that you're in?

Noelle:
It's a public pool.

Adam:
Okay, it's a public pool. And do you have any idea of where you are? Do you know where the pool is?

Noelle:
I don't know.

Adam:
Okay.

Noelle:
I don't know. I don't know.

Adam:
Okay. Do you see the end of the pool?

Noelle:
No, but I can see my family. I can see my family far away on top.

Adam:
Are you able to swim over to them?

Noelle:
Because I'm three. I don't know how to swim.

Adam:
Okay. Okay. And do you recognize your family? Do they look like the family that you have now?

Noelle:
Yes.

Adam:
Okay, and who's there? Who do you see?

Noelle:
Who do I see? I see my mom. It's my mom, my uncle, and my auntie.

Adam:
Okay. Good. You're doing really, really well. And so, are—

Noelle:
But all their backs are against me, so they can't see that I'm inside, that I'm drowning.

Adam:
Okay. As you look around the pool, do you see anywhere for you to . . . Can you float to one of the ends of the pool?

Noelle:
I can. I can.

Adam:
Okay, good. So, go ahead, and float over to . . . Find an end of the pool and float over to it. Just allow your body to be transported. Let me know when you get there.

Adam:
(Silence)

Adam:
Did you make it?

Noelle:
Okay.

Adam:
Okay, good. Good. How do you feel now?

Noelle:
I feel safe.

Adam:
Okay, good. Excellent. And so, how old would you say you are? Did you say three?

Noelle:
Three. I was three.

Adam:
Okay. Excellent, and you remember this experience.

Noelle:
Yeah.

Adam:
Okay, and what was happening? What's happening now? What do you see going on?

Noelle:
My family realized that I'm in the pool, and they're coming to save me because I have reached out to them by swimming to a safe place.

Adam:
Good.

Noelle:
Yeah.

Adam:
Good. And have they pulled you out of the pool yet, or what's—

Noelle:
Yes.

Adam:
Okay, and what are you guys doing now?

Noelle:
I woke up. I woke up, and I cry, and I feel very upset.

Adam:
Why?

Noelle:
I feel very upset that I've been abandoned. I feel that they have abandoned me, and that's why something tried to take me away.

Adam:
So, you feel like you were abandoned, and that's why something was trying to take you away.

Do you know what that something is?

Noelle:
I don't know what it is. I don't know what it is. It seems to be other spirits.

Adam:
And do you get a sense for those other spirits? Are they around you now?

Noelle:
Around me, like now?

Adam:
Can you sense them?

Noelle:
Yes.

Adam:
Okay. Okay. Okay. So, who abandoned you?

Noelle:
My parents' family, that means my mom, my auntie, and my uncle.

Adam:
Okay.

Noelle:
Yeah, that's how that happened.

Adam:
Okay.

Noelle:
There's always something that is trying to take me away, and separate me away from my family. Then I always have to try extra hard to not let them take me away.

Adam:
What do you see going on around you now? What's happening?

Noelle:
What's happening? I only see my own will to live. There's nothing. There's me, nothing else.

Adam:
Everything else went away except you?

Noelle:
Yeah, it's just me, and it's just my will to continue living in this world.

Adam:

Okay. So, Noelle, I want you to move forward to the next relevant memory. So, go ahead, and just allow yourself to be taken to the next relevant memory, wherever that is. Just allow yourself to be taken, and when you get there, let me know when you arrive.

Noelle:

It's the staircase. It's the same staircase that I went down, which you told me to.

> Note: When I induce clients into a hypnotic trance, I take them through what's called a deepener. The deepener takes them into an even deeper state of hypnosis. During the deepener, I have the client visualize a short flight of stairs as I count from ten to one. And with each number I count, the client takes a step down the stairs. By the time I get to one, the client is standing at the bottom of the staircase visualizing the hallway with many doors.

Adam:

The same staircase?

Noelle:

It's the same staircase, yeah.

Adam:

Okay.

Noelle:

I'm also three.

Adam:

Okay. And what else do you see? Can you describe what the stairs look like, and where the stairs are?

Noelle:

It's at my old house. It's at my very first house that I lived in. It's just outside my house because we live in flats, so it's like a flight of stairs. It's the same flight of stairs that came into my mind when you told me to go down.

Adam:

Okay. And so, are you in your house?

Noelle:

Yeah, it's very dark.

Adam:

Okay.

Noelle:
No, it's just outside, right outside my house, this flight of stairs. It's very dark. It's very dark. I'm alone. I'm alone. I don't know why am I alone outside the house. I'm just three. So, there's no adult. Nobody is taking care of me. I was holding an umbrella that was folded. But it's a very big umbrella, because it's too tall for my age, and something pushed me from behind, and I rolled down the stairs.

Adam:
What pushed you from behind?

Noelle:
I don't know. I can't see it.

Adam:
Okay.

Noelle:
I can't see, but it's a force. It's just something that pushed me from behind, and I rolled down the stairs into the darkness. Yeah.

Adam:
Okay. And are you able to walk up those stairs? Are you able to get up those stairs to the door?

Noelle:
I cannot. I can't. I am just lying there again.

Adam:
Okay.

Noelle:
It's the second time that it happened, that I feel very helpless. I cry really, really loudly, really, really, really loudly using all my mind. And my mom came out. She saw me. She came to save me. Yeah.

Adam:
Okay, you're doing really well.

Noelle:
And she make me safe again. She make me come back to the world again, because she doesn't want me to die. She loves me, so she's pulling me back with her love into the world.

Noelle:
Back into reality.

Adam:
From where?

Noelle:
From the darkness.

Adam:
Okay. So, where are you now?

Noelle:
I'm inside my house.

Adam:
Okay.

Noelle:
Yeah.

Adam:
And what's—

Noelle:
She make me feel, she just make me feel safe again. Telling me everything is all right.

Adam:
Good. Good. Is there anything you want to say to your mom while she's there?

Noelle:
Anything I want to say to my mom?

Noelle:
Thank you. Thank you for keeping me alive.

Adam:
And what is that darkness that you were in?

Noelle:
What is that darkness?

Noelle:
It's people that is lost spirits.

Adam:
Okay.

Noelle:
A lot of spirits who are very vengeful. It's like very thick, black smoke, very, very thick, black smoke. You can feel their hatred. You can feel how

vengeful, how all the negative emotions that they have. They are just coming for me.

Adam:
So, Noelle, here's what I'd like you to do. I'd like you to go to a memory that helps you understand why you seem to be attracted to, or go to, this place of darkness.

Noelle:
Go to a memory?

Adam:
Yeah, so just allow yourself to be moved to whatever memory is most relevant to why you're experiencing that darkness, and just allow yourself to be moved there. Don't think too hard about where to go. Just allow your soul to move to the next, most relevant experience. You're doing really well.

Noelle:
Okay.

Adam:
Okay. Where are you now?

> Note: At this point in the regression, Noelle begins to relive memories from past lives.

Noelle:
It's someplace that I couldn't really recognize. It's not the present time.

Adam:
Okay, good.

Noelle:
It's a past time.

Adam:
Okay, good. And what are you seeing? What are your impressions?

Noelle:
It's probably the ancient Chinese time, but I don't know when. Yeah, I'm a kept woman.

Adam:
What does that mean?

Noelle:
So, that means I'm not a proper lady during that time.

Adam:

Okay. Okay, and what's going on where you are? What's the scene?

Noelle:

There's a lot of entertainment. There's a lot of entertainment. There's a lot of men, and I'm serving the men. Yeah, and there's a lot of like music, people playing, like orchestra. The men are drunk. We were being brought in to entertain them, and there's a lot of money. And in me, in me there's a lot of grit. It's very superficial. We have to put on an act to associate ourself with them, so that we can be rich, and be powerful. Yeah. Yeah. But it's something that we do against our will. Yeah, and it's chasing. It's always chasing. We want more and more money. We want to be the most richest lady. So, that the one with the highest rank will pick us.

Adam:

Do you get a sense for how old you are?

Noelle:

Early twenties, and it's very bad, because I've done a lot of things to make it.

Adam:

What kinds of things?

Noelle:

It includes like when I get really, really jealous of the other ladies, and I will spread rumors about them. I will destroy their belongings. I bullied toward them. I bullied them. I make them really, really very . . . I've hurt them a lot. I gang up with other ladies against them. I even use magic against them.

Adam:

Okay. You're doing really good. This is important.

Noelle:

Yeah. Yeah. Yeah, so probably in this life, they are coming to find me, to seek revenge. They just feel very vengeful.

Adam:

So, why don't we do this. Let's do this, Noelle. Why don't you move forward to your next relevant memory in that lifetime?

Noelle:

In that lifetime?

Adam:
Yes. So, just continue to just move to the next most relevant memory. Let me know when you're there.

Noelle:
In that same lifetime?

Adam:
Yeah, or just wherever you go to next. Just allow yourself to be . . . Let's keep exploring that theme though.

Noelle:
Okay.

Adam:
Where are you now?

Noelle:
But it seems to be another era.

Adam:
Okay, good.

Noelle:
It seems to be more . . . It's probably during a wartime. I don't know when. During a wartime. I'm at the train station, and I have to be separated from the man I love. He's on the train. He has to leave. I don't know why. And then the train just leave the station. I'm left behind again, and my heart is breaking. I just feel that something seems to be taking him away from me because I threw away things from other people before.

Adam:
So, Noelle, why don't you go to a memory that will help you to understand what kinds of things were happening, what kinds of things you took away.

Noelle:
What kind of things I took away?

Adam:
Yeah, like when you say you took from people, and that's why you feel you're being taken away from. If you're able to go to a memory that helps you understand why you feel that way.

Noelle:
Because I used to, by being in that kind of work, I've broken families up.

Adam:
Okay. Okay.

Noelle:
Yeah, so I broke families up. I have broken real love between people. So, this is the same thing that's happening to me when my loved ones will eventually leave, or eventually leave me. And then I'll be helpless. There's nothing much that I can do, but only with their love, the true love of people around me whenever, no matter in which lifetime, that can pull me back, and help me to continue to live here in each lifetime, again and again. This love doesn't have to come from people. It can be from a higher being, but I must avow myself. I must value myself, and love on myself to let them in.

Adam:
To let the higher beings in?

Noelle:
To let this love in. It can be from any Source because this love doesn't discriminate. It's the purest form of confession in love. It's the same Source. So, your mom's love to you. Your son's love to you. A husband's love to you. It manifests from the same Source.

Adam:
So, Noelle, I want you to feel that love. I want you to feel that love move through your body, and as you feel that love, that radiating love through your entire body, I want you to allow it to move you to a memory, or to an experience that you feel really connected with that love.

Noelle:
It's after I've given birth, and the first time that I've seen my son. The first time when I see my son.

> Note: At this point within the regression, Noelle is taken back to an experience from her present life when she gave birth to her son. It's here that she is able to reconnect with Source energy.

Adam:
Okay.

Noelle:
It's that kind of love, and it's radiating out from me. I can't control it. It's just very natural. It's the purest form of love, and I think it seems to ... It doesn't seem to be coming just from me alone. So, it's like seems to be connected to a higher being that is shining the love through me. And I

think it seems to be the same for everyone. This Source of love is coming from the same Source, but you know that. Yeah. Yeah.

Adam:
And are you able to get a sense of if that Source is with you right now where you are?

Noelle:
Yes.

Adam:
Okay.

Noelle:
Yes.

Adam:
Okay, good.

Noelle:
Yeah, it's still very strong.

Adam:
Okay, and do you see the Source? Do you sense it? What is your experience with it right now?

Noelle:
It's in my body. It's inside me, and it's making me do. I just feel very warm. I just feel very warm again. There is no room for thinking.

Adam:
Good.

Noelle:
There's no room for thinking. You just talk. You don't think about what you're saying. You don't know why you're talking, but it seems to be the truth, but you don't have to rationalize it. It's just a Source of love, and it's like the human body is just a bridge. It's really just a bridge to reflect this Source of love that you need to be connected to it. You need to focus. You can't rationalize. You can't think too much. You can't try to make sense of it. It's just there. And to feel it, you must have clarity. You don't feel it with your brain. You feel it with your heart. Yeah?

Adam:
Yes. So, Noelle, I want you to connect with that love—

Noelle:
This Source of light is trying to communicate it, that a force . . . It's trying

to shine light to the dark force, so that they will feel better, so that they can see. So, that the darkness can see this Source of light as well. Yeah, and that's why this seems to be keeping me alive. Yeah.

Adam:
So, Noelle, while you're there with that energy Source, I want you to ask it a couple of questions. And it may not—

Noelle:
I'm here, just right beside him, yeah.

Adam:
Okay, excellent. Excellent. So, you see Source now?

Noelle:
Yeah.

Adam:
Good, okay. So, one of the questions that you had from your near-death experience is why are you still here? And why did you come back into your body?

Noelle:
I know. I know it now. Because the light doesn't want me to give up on myself.

Adam:
Good.

Noelle:
The light, there is still this love. You remember? Remember?

Adam:
Yeah.

Noelle:
When there's love, when there's love, it's what keeps you alive, this compassion and this love. And once you allow it to enter into your life, you can't leave. You just can't. You can't leave this world. It will help you to overcome anything. Your time is just not. It's just not due because the light is still with you here on earth, here on earth itself. Yeah.

Adam:
So, do you want to ask Source how you can heal from what you're going through now?

Noelle:
Noelle asks, "How can I heal?"

It's to connect to this Source, and make it bigger, like to reconnect with the Source, and make the light bigger, so that it can show the darkness this light and make them understand. Make them understand by experiencing the light to make sense of what they are experiencing as well, so that they can let go. So that they can also feel this energy, and let go of what has happened, and transform. Yeah.

Adam:
You mentioned that in this lifetime, you've experienced so many ups and downs, and pain and suffering. Why have you gone through so much?

Noelle:
It's something that I've done in the past coming too. All these disruptions are being caused by them coming to take me away from my family time and time again. So, this is why I have so many disruptions to my life, and I need to connect with the Source. I found it really. I just need to really connect to the Source, and show them the light. Show them the light.

Adam:
Is that why they're coming to you? Is that why these beings are coming after you? Because they're attracted to the light?

Noelle:
They are coming to me because I've hurt them before. They are very vengeful, so it means they are honest, near-death experiences, and all the disruptions, they are just coming back to me because I've used magic on them before. So, that is like a passage where they can come through that to try to harm me, and take away my life, and pay them back in this life. But I'm being kept here because of them. There's love and compassion from this being of light, which is all around me. And it's telling me there is no differentiation of the quality of love no matter whether it is from a stranger, from your son, or from whoever. It's the same. It's the same Source. So, I have to grow it, so that this darkness can understand, and it can let go, and not be so vengeful. Yeah. Yeah.

Adam:
That's powerful! So, maybe this goes in connection with what you shared, but you mentioned that you have a genetic disease. You have a problem at the DNA level, which made your body a little bit physically different from normal, and you wanted to know why you were different. Is that something you want to ask?

Noelle:
Yeah. Yeah. Because I have to be.

Noelle asks, "Why am I different?" I'm asking it, "Why am I different?"

Because they say that "if you are not different, you will not feel me." Yeah. "You won't be able to sense me, and have my protection." That's what the light told me. That's all. Yeah.

Adam:
Good. So, Noelle, I know you also, that you have a very special connection with your son, and you wanted to know why that connection is so strong, or how is that connection so strong.

Noelle:
It's that I can feel the light through him. I can feel the light through him. He is a mirror of. He is like a mirror. I think that the light can shine through me from the Source, through me to him, and from him back to me. Yeah. And he is supposed to show me the way. I don't know why he's supposed to show me the way.

Adam:
That's great.

Noelle:
He's supposed to show me the way. I don't know how. I don't know why. Yeah.

Adam:
Okay, good.

Noelle:
Okay.

Adam:
Good. So, Noelle, you also mentioned that you keep seeing the angel numbers, 1111. Is there a message that you're supposed to be getting from those numbers?

Noelle:
I don't know yet.

Adam:
Okay.

Noelle:
I don't know yet. I don't know.

Adam:
Is the light able to answer?

Noelle:
No.

Adam:
So, Noelle, can you ask the light why you were shown the memories from your current life and past lives today?

Noelle:
It's to make the connection of taking away, and being taken away from somebody. And now, losing it is to make the connection, because when I was at a different point during the first few memories, I feel like I've been abandoned. I feel like they, my loved ones, abandoned me, but it's not. The truth is that because . . . So, for the last three memories, I always feel that I've been un-cared for. I've been abandoned, and that's why all this happened. So, at the train station, I couldn't understand why. Why does he have to leave? Why is it that the circumstance is like that? Then during the incident, I couldn't understand why my family couldn't see me drowning. When I fell down the stairs, I wonder why did my mom not pay more attention to me? In the past life, I saw that I have been the cause, and I've broken up people's love, and family, and that is what is happening. So, that is the answer of why.

Adam:
Okay. And can you ask how you heal that karma? How do you—
(Noelle interjects)

Noelle:
The light. The light. The light has really told me I need to grow. I need to grow it bigger. I don't know how. I know how I can grow it bigger, but I need to show the darkness. Because they are at a very dark place. They can't feel anything. All they can feel is just a vengefulness. They need to see, and they need to let go. Yeah. Yes. Yeah.

Adam:
Is there anything else, Noelle, that you want to explore while you're here with the light?

Noelle:
It is actually following me wherever I go. And it is following everybody wherever they go. It's just that, whether is it burning bright or it is very dim. And some people just ignore it. Some people just ignore it. But if you connect back to the Source of this light, you will know everything. You will just know. Yeah. And I want to tell you, it has a message for you. People that you know already that have passed on, they are still with you.

They are forever with you. They are not gone just like that. They don't really disappear, but they are with you. Not in person, but together as a Source.

Adam:
Thank you.

Noelle:
Yeah, that's all.

Adam:
Thank you.

Noelle:
Okay.

Adam:
Anything else, Noelle, that you want to explore while you're here in this space?

Noelle:
No, that's all.

CHAPTER VIII

CARLA

I met Carla shortly after posting on social media a call for volunteers for the NDE regression research. Not long after Carla reached out via private message, she and I spoke over the phone about her NDE. She prefaced her story by saying that she wasn't sure if her experience counted as "near-death," but she was sure it was an out-of-body experience.

Carla's account is much different than any of the other accounts in this book. In fact, it's different than most of the accounts I've read. Carla wasn't ill. She wasn't seen by physicians. There was nothing biological about her near-death experience. With that said, I invite you to read her incredible NDE account and regression transcription.

Carla's NDE Account

Carla: The out-of-body experience I had happened when I was maybe nineteen, but it relates back to what was going on when I was fifteen. At fifteen, I got pregnant by a brother of a friend of mine. He was twenty-one, and I was fifteen. And it was consensual as far as a fifteen-year-old can make any decisions about that kind of thing. But I got pregnant and I didn't know—I assumed since he was older and more experienced that he would be taking care of that, and, of course, that didn't happen—so there was this big scene where I'm telling my parents that I'm pregnant and I made this guy Jeff come with me because I didn't want to face them by myself.

My mother was pretty horrible. She called me a whore and she wanted to know where I had checked, where I got the pregnancy test. And so I told her and she says,

"You didn't use your real name, did you?"

So I said, "Yeah," And she went crazy, because that means that other people would know, since my father was a physician and all the physicians were in a group, and that other people would know that her daughter was pregnant.

So that really upset her and that her plans for me and my wedding were now shot. And so all of that unpleasantness and, of course, I'm an immigrant. So we were doing all of this in Spanish, right, and Jeff didn't speak any Spanish, so he was going, "Well, what are they saying? What are they saying?" I'm having to interpret into English (laughs) while being beaten up by my mother verbally. So, it was quite a hysterical scene in both senses of the word hysterical. Funny and not funny. And so then my parents threw Jeff out of the house and said don't ever see our daughter again or we will come after you for statutory rape. And then I said I wanted an abortion because I was fifteen, and I didn't want a child to be raised by my mother. I mean that I knew I would turn into my mother if I had a child. So, that the whole idea of abusing another child to that extent just wiped me out. And back then there wasn't the open adoption and some of the other possibilities. Abortion was illegal in Kansas, so my parents did step up and help me get that abortion.

We had to fly, my mother and I flew to New York. And we went into this one place . . . and oh, on the way to New York, I remember looking out the airplane window and in the middle of all of this misery, there was a big cloud that had lightning flashing in it. And it was so beautiful. So incredibly beautiful. So I took great strength from that.

And then, you know, I have five brothers and sisters and they were all given wrong information about where we were going and what was going on. So I had no support. And also, as soon as my parents found out, we moved out of that community. So I lost all my friends. I lost all connection.

So we went to New York. And the first place that we went to, I was stripped and laying down and my legs up and, you know, open and waiting. And finally this guy comes in. Some kind of doctor or health provider and he doesn't say hello. He doesn't give me any eye contact. He just shoves his finger in, feels around on my belly, and then says, "God damn it!" and leaves.

So then a nurse comes in and says, "You can get dressed." And so it turns out that I was too far gone—too many weeks into the pregnancy for the kind of abortion they did, so we had to make plans to go to another clinic. And then I had this Rh factor. That if I ever got pregnant again, it could hurt the child. So there are all these logical things I had to do while dealing with my mother's, you know, spreading shame. Shaming me the whole time.

So that finished, we got back, and, when I was about eighteen, my mother tells me that she needed to talk to me. She says,

"Jeff committed suicide about a year ago. I didn't tell you about it because I didn't want your schoolwork affected. But now that you've been accepted into college I can tell you. And oh, by the way, he's been writing you letters. He had been writing you letters, which I destroyed."

So, I went into very high level of emotion, ran out of the house, and went into nature, where I usually go to get grounded again. All of this to explain the whole emotional background on this. Her betrayal and his killing himself and my wondering, you know my taking on the guilt of him killing himself and now I have blood on my hands from two humans—Jeff and the baby. So, I'm carrying all of this inside of me trying to just shove it down, I guess. And I'm in college. And I'm living in a co-op where there are a lot of people. I have a lot of social life. I'm intellectually very challenged and am just enjoying college and learning and just eating it all up, all the different experiences. Finally freed of my family home and my parents, though they paid for my education, and I appreciate that.

Oh, so, at this time, I have a boyfriend. He's a beautiful man. A beautiful, sweet, tender fellow and a musician. And he takes me to a movie, *Harold and Maude*, and it's about suicide, and so, in the middle of the movie, I have a meltdown and run outside. I'm sobbing. I hide in some alley in some corner. He comes out; he finds me. He's very sweet with me and takes me back to the house, the cooperative housing where we both lived. And so I tell him the story of Jeff and how he killed himself. He had done it with a gun which I had seen. He had shown me the gun before. Jeff had shown me the gun before back when I was fifteen. And when I saw it, I thought it was a toy gun, and I held it up, and when I went, "Bang! Bang!" towards him, and he got freaked out, because, of course, it was a real gun and apparently loaded.

So, Charlie, my college boyfriend at the time, after he hears all of this he says, "Okay. This is what we're going to do. We're going to go back to Topeka where this happened." And we were living in Austin where we were going to school.

"We're going to drive up there, and we're going to find his grave and you're at least going to be able to grieve for him at his grave."

So I said, "Okay that's a good plan."

So we get in his car, but by this time—we went for a weekend—and by this time, I'm in a state of mind where I'm not really functioning. Well, I don't have memories really from that whole trip except that I just trusted Charlie so much. I just gave him all of the decision-making power, and he would just tell me go sit down, go do this. So we somehow, I don't know how, he figured it out, got to the cemetery and the plot.

And what I remember is getting out of the car and he says, "This is the grave right here." And I'm walking toward it. And when I see the headstone, "Jeff Jackson," I fall on my knees, and I start sobbing with grief. So, that was when I left my body. And I, which is not this body, but I, who is not even this identity so much. It's just some innermost, the innermost light of me went into this area that was not dark, not really brilliant light, but just kind of a gray infinite area above and below in all directions. I wasn't afraid of it—I was curious. I wasn't in the midst of the emotions anymore. I was just kind of hanging out and thinking, "Wow!" And then I see a light coming. There was a little light that became a big light, and my interpretation was that it was far away and it came closer and closer. And it could have been little and just gotten big, but there's no distance. I mean that there was a distance between us but there was no way to measure it. You know, was it three hundred thousand miles or an inch? Or, how big was I? None of those things mattered in this situation. So, as it got closer or bigger, I started recognizing Jeff, but it was not just the Jeff I knew. It was Jeff as—I don't know how to explain it—it was Jeff as all of his incarnations. He was so much more complex and had so much more to his personality than the Jeff I knew. I mean the Jeff I knew was there. The basic Jeff was the Jeff I knew. But then there was all this other stuff, of stuff he had done, and people he had been, and his wisdom was much higher than it ever was in life in this planet. And so I was very happy to see him.

And there is a conversation that happened without words. It was at that time—I remember describing it well back when I ended up telling Charlie. You know, some time later, what happened? I described it as a liquid—a warm liquid that flowed from back and forth between Jeff and I, that was full of information. So, there were no words, but there were feelings of how much he loved me. That it wasn't my fault. That he was definitely okay. I mean, he didn't even have to say that because I could just feel it. I was okay. There was no reason for me to carry this guilt around anymore. So, it was such a huge experience, but I had no way to know how much time that took. It seemed to finish. It seemed like it was complete.

Then, the communication was complete, and I felt my knees on the ground, my body hunched over, the liquid snot and tears on my face and hands, and I look up and Charlie's coming. And I asked him how long has it been. He says twenty minutes. That he had been walking around giving me time to do whatever I needed to do. So, we got in the car and headed back home.

There were two gifts from this experience that I haven't even really talked to you about:

No fear of death. In fact, I long for death, because it really seems like it's going to be you know—this is a veil of tears here, and where I'm going will be home, and it will be a place where I belong and there's unconditional love. And I'm so sure of that, that sometimes I even get jealous when I hear somebody's got a fatal disease, I think, "Oh, shit! They got to go. I still have to stay here." But you know, I've made my peace with that there must be a reason for me to be here. For a purpose. And that there's still some good that I can do. Okay, so that was one gift—no fear of death.

And another was the taking away of the guilt. You know, it didn't go away a hundred percent, because I would still fall into that mindset every now and then, but it was very light and temporal. You know temporary. If I was in a bad shape for other reasons, for the rest of my life, that guilt may come up. But not too much for him, but for the baby.

After we wrapped recording Carla's NDE account, she shared a few questions that she wanted to cover during her regression session.

- Is the baby I lost as a child OK?
- Is there any connection between my step-grandchildren and the baby I lost?

In our regression session, I took Carla into a hypnotic state and then set the intention for her to experience whatever serves her soul's greatest good as it related to her NDE. The following is a transcript of Carla's regression session.

Carla's NDE Regression

After getting Carla into a deeply relaxed hypnotic trance, I asked her to use her powerful imagination to visualize a hallway with many doors, with each of the doors representing an experience or a set of memories from her life. I then asked Carla to find a door that seemed to stand out from the others and walk up to it. Once Carla arrived at the door, she let me know by saying, "I'm here." Then, I connected Carla with the intention that we set for the regression and asked her to walk through the door. The below is a verbatim transcription of Carla's regression session.

* Carla walks through the door—

Adam:
Carla, please tell me what you're seeing.

Carla:
Space.

Adam:
Okay. What—

Carla:
White.

Adam:
Okay.

Carla:
White, like diffuse light a little bit in the distance, not a particular person's spirit but like a group or a force.

Adam:
Okay.

Carla:
I'm drawn toward the light. It's curious but also just so, so much love and so much peace. Home. Belonging. I can't tell the individuals, but I'm part of this group. They open for me and surround me and hold me and I am so grateful. It's as though there are so many hands and hands of light soothing me. I can't make out faces or individual identities, just relaxing into the light, the welcoming. Bienvenido is the Spanish word for welcome, and my grandfather was named that, and I feel is the welcoming, and he's mixed in with this.

Adam:
Do you want to ask who the group is? Are you able to ask?

Carla:
Yeah.

Carla asks, "Who are you? Who is this group?"

Oh, well, I don't know. I don't know but I just feel so much connection and so much love, so much missing them. I've been missing them.

Carla asks, "Who is this group?"

It's a family group, a kind of family, a kind of community, goes way back. We know each other from way, way back. I'm so glad to see everybody. To see, to be here. Oh, they're just infusing me with more relaxation and love, as though they're trying to calm me or fill me, fill up an emptiness I had felt. I need to do this first to be present with them. I need to accept it, open to it.

Adam:
You need to open and accept what in particular, Carla?

Carla:
Their relationship to me. My relationship to them, that I wasn't forgotten. A lot of sorrow. I feel a lot of sorrow, but I still don't see anybody in particular. It's this whole group and . . . (Silence)

Adam:
Okay. That's good. You're doing really well.

Carla:
I want to see my baby.

Adam:
Okay. Do you want to ask if your baby's soul can come forward from that group?

Carla:
"Can the baby's soul come forward, please?"

Oh. Yes. Feels like a, she's like a small package of light that just cuddles up against my chest. And I'm expressing my guilt, my sorrow, my love, and she's fine. She's fine. She feels my love. She's okay. She's still so tiny. It's like she melts into me, into my light, and we become brighter and I'm whole, more whole.

Carla:
And I see a teenager, a smiling teenager, shy and proud, and I hold my arms out and she comes forward. Pink, pink rosy skin and bright brown eyes and curly hair and her front luminous.

Adam:
Do you know who that is?

Carla:
It's her.

Adam:
Oh.

Carla:
It's who I've been calling Mariposa, butterfly.

Adam:
You're doing great, Carla, just breathe.

Carla:
I've missed you so much. I've missed you so much. She's calm. She's happy. It's okay with her that I'm all emotional. She understands. She's okay. There's just love.

Adam:
Just enjoy the experience, Carla. You're right where you're supposed to be.

Carla:
We're sitting cross-legged across from each other, and the whole group surrounds us in a ball of light, and we're in the center and they're humming, they're singing, they're vibrating, and we're holding hands, both hands and just looking in each other's eyes, and her face isn't clear but I see the eyes and they're looking at me, and there's still shame from my side that's preventing . . . I want to let go of the shame. Not my fault, but also part of what I planned.

Adam:
Did you want to ask your daughter what the plan was? Why—
(Carla interjects)

> Note: There are some who believe that before we incarnate, we make a life plan. In that life plan, we pick our parents, friends, and our purpose for the upcoming incarnation. In this example, Carla asks her daughter about why Carla had the abortion and why her daughter's soul volunteered to play that role.

Carla:
Okay. Here's what she said, "I had a past life as a male and I committed suicide and my mother, in that life, was very . . . was destroyed from that, her pain and somehow having to let go of my daughter was connected to that."

Adam:
It's almost karma to live out.

Carla:
I wanted to understand what she felt. So I thank Mariposa for being willing to act that out with me, to work that out with me. I asked her if she was that woman, and she said no, she wasn't my mother in that life. But we've been connected forever, seems like. She's like my sister.

Adam:
Did you want to ask her if there's any connection between your step-grandchildren and her?

Carla:
I'm afraid to ask. I'm afraid to ask. I don't know where the fear is coming from.

Adam:
Okay.

Carla:
Why am I afraid to ask? I'm afraid to ask because maybe there is no connection. Well, why? Why do I want that connection so much? Because I miss Mariposa. I want to be giving to her and she says it's, giving is giving. Giving to a baby is giving to a baby. It doesn't really matter who's who. I'm too attached or too insistent that it be her. That my love should be broader than that, more complete if I could love the one you're with. Love the opportunity you're given. That's where you love and that she'll be with me.

Adam:
You're doing really well.

Carla:
That's part of the sorrow, the sorrow of that mother was there was no other son. She only had one son, and when I killed myself in my past life, she lost it all.

Adam:
Carla, are you able to understand why you killed yourself in that past life? Are you able to ask that question?

Carla:
Oh, yeah. Yeah, that's a past life I've explored before.

Adam:
Okay. Okay.

Carla:
I had joined up in a war to be a man because I felt like I had to be a man. I didn't have a father and . . . then I got . . . I was a prisoner of war and I was tortured, and I was finally released but I couldn't handle the damage done to me because of that torture, and I finally ended it all. And I knew that I was going to hurt my mother, but I just couldn't bear it anymore. Yeah.

Adam:
So do you get a sense, Carla, about where you are? And are you able to see anyone any more clearly?

Carla:
Yeah, I start seeing hair and facial but I don't . . . I still feel the presence of my grandfather somewhere.

Adam:
Did you want to ask and see if your grandfather would make his presence known?

Carla:
Bienvenido, okay, he's in front of me and he's taking my hands, and he's just letting me know he loves me. He loved me when I was a little girl. I only saw him before I was five. Oh, oh, (sigh) I didn't have grandparents because of the situation, and so I want to be a grandparent now, and that's part of my own healing is for me to be a grandparent and to give. And I knew I had missed something, but I am now experiencing more of what that missing entailed. And he missed it too.

Carla:
So I see my grandmother who was his wife and I apologized to her. Because I did see her later, when I was about thirteen, and wasn't very nice to her. But she understands. It was just a lot of loss that I went through. And I am like her in a lot of ways, and she knows that, and she sends me love and songs. She made up songs, and she sends me my own

*songs, helps me make my own songs, and she knows I'm making them
and she is proud of that.*

Carla:
*What about my other grandparents? My mother's parents? They're in the
back, way in the back, dark shadows there. I don't know.*

Adam:
Can you ask them to come forward?

Carla:
Josefina, Gustavo. Thank God.

Adam:
Were they able to come or are they . . .

Carla:
Yeah, it's, communication is difficult.

Adam:
Okay.

Carla:
*It appears that what I had surmised is correct, but my grandmother . . .
See they both died when my mother was a teenager, so there was no
getting to know them. And then we left Cuba and left all connection
to them behind, in terms of objects or places. So I asked if Josefina, the
grandmother, what was the problem between her and my mother? Why
was there so much secrecy from my mother's part? Was it like my father
said, that it was just her death was so traumatic or was there something
before that?*

Carla:
*I'm not sure if she's ashamed that she did something wrong with my
mother. She blames herself, and she's happy that I've worked on it
through therapy and stuff so it won't keep going down through the
generations. I don't know exactly what it was, maybe some depression.
Maybe she was very, very depressed and was unable to give my mother
what she needed.*

Carla:
*So my mother is coming forward, and she and I have patched things too
through earlier work that was done after she died. I don't really see faces.
I just sense them and see outlines of light and I feel their love and . . . So
my grandfather is not so involved with me. That's okay.*

Adam:
Your grandfather on your mother's side?

Carla:
Right.

Adam:
Okay.

Carla:
He gave her lots of love, and that love that he gave her, she was able to give to me. So that was a good ancestor thread. But he's distracted. He's supposed to be somewhere else. Yeah, he's not somebody I could relate to. He's really into making money or something. Oh, yeah, it's okay. It's okay. There's peace between us.

Carla:
And I'm grateful for my grandmother, the maternal grandmother. She's tiny and dark haired, or maybe a veil. Maybe she's wearing a veil. And my mother is, her eyes are shiny. She's glad and she's encouraging my grandmotherness, to pass on love. That's the important thing. Yeah. Yeah. Yeah, so I asked her, is it true that these grandkids don't really have anything to do with my baby and she says, "Yeah, that's true."

Adam:
That they don't have anything to do with your son?

Carla:
Right. (Silence)

Carla:
I mean, they're not the same soul.

Adam:
That sounds like the purpose. They're sharing with you that your purpose is to pass your love on to your grandchildren.

Carla:
Yeah. Yeah. Yeah. So I will. I will. So why was . . . can I keep asking them questions?

Adam:
Yeah, yeah, this is your time. You can ask whatever you want, Carla.

Carla:
"So why did Angie get pregnant all those times when she didn't mean to get pregnant?"

Well, she's got her path, things she's got to learn. That she wanted to learn. And I'm just lucky to be there so that I can help her. It works out for me.

Adam:
And who is Angie? Is that your stepdaughter?

Carla:
Yeah, Angie is a stepdaughter, yeah.

Adam:
All right.

Carla:
She's not here. We're just talking about her.

Adam:
Yep.

Carla:
My mother knew Angie for a little bit.

"So is there anything else that this community of mine here can give me?"

That their love is always available. I just need to tune into it. They know I'm tired and that I want to rest, but there's still things for me to do here and I shouldn't give up. Death will happen when it's supposed to happen, when I'm finished and finishing has to do with loving.

Carla:
I'd like to ask for my ex-husbands to come forth. John, John Kingston.

Nobody's seen him. No, he's not ready. He's not ready yet. Jeff, I just want to thank you one more time.

Adam:
Did you want to call Jeff forward?

Carla:
Yeah, I see him. He's way in the back. He's just a light and I'm thanking him and he's receiving it and grinning, the light equivalent of grinning. He's glad I'm with my people here. Is there anything else I should know about my siblings?

My father, I don't see him here either. No. He's here but distant.

What's with that? Huh?

My father is not here and my grandfather is not, on one side anyway.

Adam:
Did you want to ask your mom?

Carla:
Okay. He's healing. She says he's healing. Give him time. Okay. So my siblings, they're all still alive. She's proud of them. She's glad that everybody's doing well.

Carla:
There's one whose brain has an illness. I know which one she's talking about, but that she says I'm right to notice that his heart, his emotional side, his loving side is becoming more apparent and that it's good that I notice that and reflect that back to him and not try too much to connect on the cognitive side. (Silence)

Carla:
No. She thanks me for coming up with the idea of doing the Zoom since the pandemic began with all the siblings and any other relative we can snare. That she's present during those times and is very pleased that we are gathered in love. And they're gone. It's time for me to come back, I guess.

CHAPTER IX

KRISTEN

I met Kristen in 2020 at a networking event. Kristen is a psychic medium who teaches people how to develop their own intuitive gifts and abilities. When Kristen learned that I was conducting this research, she asked if she could volunteer.

Not only does Kristen have an NDE story—she has four of them. If you're new to NDEs, it might sound odd that someone would have multiple near-death experiences. However, it's not uncommon for people to have multiple NDEs.

Kristen's NDE Account

Kristen: So my first near-death experience. I was a small child. I don't remember exactly what age, but somewhere between the age of five and seven, I died as a result of child abuse and related head injury. All I remember about my out-of-body experience is walking across a meadow, you know, there was long grass. And of course I was tiny because I was little, but the grass was tall, the flowers were big, and there was a boulder on the other side of the meadow. And I just kept walking toward the boulder, and when I got there, I realized that there was a man there sitting on a rock and, as I got closer, I realized that that man was Jesus and he looked like Bob Marley.

I was a little confused at first being raised, you know, in a traditional white Christian church. But Jesus helped me climb up onto the rock, and we just sat there and we talked a while. I don't remember anything that we talked about, until he said it's time to go back. And I didn't realize really what was happening. But he helped me down off the rock, said he would see me again, and I walked back across the meadow. By this time I was almost all the way back. But there was a tree I hadn't seen before and the tree went up. It was tall. I don't know how to judge its height, but it was pretty far up and then split into two and my eyes followed it up to the tallest point, where I couldn't see the top of the tree. And then I distinctly remember my vision coming back down towards the tree split and going up the other side, and I could see the top on the other side. It was shorter. And then, just like that, I was back in my body, lying on the floor with nobody around. That was what I remember from my first near-death experience.

My next one. I was fourteen and I OD'd and was in the hospital. I was really deep into the throes of addiction at that point, and I had a bowel rupture because I hadn't been eating, and I had been drinking and popping pills for days; it paralyzed me. I was then taken into the emergency room and I was screaming in pain. And at the hospital, I remember some guy with a flowered surgical hat trying to get me undressed to get me into a hospital gown. And I came to at that moment, somehow managed to swing at him, and I popped him in the jaw. I think the shock caused him to fly backward. And then I remember my mom coming in and helping me get my hospital gown on. After that, I was in a coma for four days. And during that time on the other side, I saw a staircase, which I walked up. And on the left side of the top of the staircase was a door with a bright light coming out from it.

I kept knocking on the door and saying, "I'm here let me in!" And there was a voice on the other side saying, "It's not your time. You have to go back." And apparently for four days that conversation was going on. I was arguing—I had no intention of going back, but eventually I ended up back in my body and came out of the coma.

My next near-death experience happened when I was in labor with my first child, and it had been a difficult pregnancy. I was on my second day of hard labor and my heart stopped, and I wasn't gone very long. But because I'd already experienced death a couple of times, I knew what was happening, and I felt myself starting to lift out of my body. At that point, my consciousness took over and said that I have a baby to raise, I can't leave now. So, I pulled myself back into my body, but I never really got all the way out in the first place. I just felt it coming.

My fourth and last NDE was six years ago. I had a severe case of pneumonia and my lungs were being crushed by all the fluid in my cavity, and I couldn't breathe, and at one point I just went, "Okay, I'm ready." And I made a conscious decision to just let go of my body and this time I was going to walk through that door that I described in my second NDE. The door to the left of the stairway. And so I did. I walked into this beautiful, bright light and it just was the most profound love and peace I could ever have imagined. Thinking back on it, I felt the same profound love and peace during my first NDE when I was sitting on the rock with Jesus. But in this experience, I was just in this beautiful bright white light. I couldn't see anything, but I could feel so much. And then I heard my husband's voice, and I got sucked backwards through the door and back into my body. And that's it. Other than I was really pissed off to be back in my body.

Adam: Understood, Kristen. In your fourth NDE, were you able to see whose voice it was you were hearing? Did you see Jesus when you walked through the door?

Kristen: Not when I walked through the door. I just felt pure love and joy and it was just brilliant white light.

Adam: Did you get a sense or a feeling that Jesus was present in your last NDE?

Kristen: If Jesus was there, he was there not as an entity. He was in my first experience, but not in NDEs two, three, and four.

Adam: So, Jesus was only visually present during NDE number one?

Kristen: Yep, you know, I don't know who the voice was on the other side of the door. It may have been him. I'm not sure. What the first NDE taught me, though, was, because again, I grew up in an excessively violent home, I learned that I could leave my body and not experience what was happening to my body. Because I would just go back to that meadow and hang out on the rock. And sometimes I would talk to Jesus, but then it was like a choice. It was more like a meditative state than an out-of-body. And when the abuse was over, I would go back. And I did that throughout my childhood once I learned how.

After we wrapped recording Kristen's NDE account, she shared a few questions that she wanted to cover during her regression session.

- What was the conversation with Jesus about in NDE 1?
- Who was the voice on the other side of the door in NDE 2?
- Why did I choose to come back after NDE 4?

In our regression session, I took Kristen into a hypnotic state and then set the intention for her to experience whatever serves her soul's greatest good as it related to her NDE. The following is a transcript of Kristen's regression session.

Kristen's NDE Regression

Kristen's hypnotic induction was conducted differently than all of the other volunteers for this study. As you'll read in her account, in two of Kristen's NDEs, she saw a staircase and at the top of a staircase was a door that wouldn't open. I decided to use that as the hypnotic deepener visualization that led her into the regression. Instead of visualizing a hallway with many doors, I asked her to visualize the staircase she experienced in her NDE. And as I counted up from one to ten, with each number I counted, Kristen took a step up the stairs. Once Kristen arrived at the door at the top of the staircase, she let me know by saying, "I'm here." Then, I connected Kristen with the intention that we set for the regression and asked her to walk through the door. The below is a verbatim transcription of Kristen's regression session.

* Kristen walks through the door—

Adam:
Kristen, please tell me, what are you seeing?

Kristen:
Right now, I'm not seeing anything.

Adam:
Okay.

Kristen:
There's kind of vague colors floating around. (Silence)

Kristen:
Purple, red.

Adam:
Excellent. Excellent. And what does it feel like? What are the feelings or the emotions?

Kristen:
Relaxed. A little bit of apprehension. *(Silence)*

Kristen:
It's not what I expected. *(Silence)*

Kristen:
There's a lot of purple. *(Silence)*

Adam:
If you look down, are you able to see if you have anything on your feet, or are you wearing anything on your feet?

Kristen:
All I can see is purple.

Adam:
Okay.

Kristen:
There's a little bit of white in the middle of it now.

Adam:
Is there? Okay.

Kristen:
Yeah.

Adam:
And what does the white look like? Is it a specific shape?

Kristen:
It's just like a pinpoint of light that's fading in and out.

Adam:
Okay, great. Perhaps follow the light. Can you get closer to it?

Kristen:
Colors just keep moving, like swirl, not swirling like in a circle, but just moving around all over.

Adam:
Okay. And what does this place feel like? Does it feel familiar? Is it new? What are you getting?

Kristen:
It feels like I'm just in an empty space.

Adam:
Okay. All right. And do you get the sense that there's anyone else there?

And when I say anyone, it doesn't have to be a human, but is there a feeling of anyone else around?

Kristen:
My dog from childhood just came running up.

Adam:
Oh, what's your dog's name?

Kristen:
Laddie. He's a collie.

Adam:
Excellent. Excellent. And are you able to ask him where you are?

Kristen:
He said to follow him.

Adam:
Okay. So go ahead and follow him and see where he takes you.

Kristen:
I'm a little girl, and I'm riding him like I used to. And I'm holding onto his fur and he's running.

Adam:
And where is he taking you? What do you see around you now?

Kristen:
It's brighter now. He took me back to the field that I went to in my NDE. The flowers, wildflowers, and the long grasses.

Adam:
So you're seeing flowers and grass around you now?

Kristen:
Yeah.

Adam:
And what does it feel like where you are?

Kristen:
I can hear water running, like a river or a creek or something, off to my left, and it's just sunshine, and it's this big field and I am still little. The grass is about as tall as I am.

Kristen:
He's taking me over to talk to Jesus again.

Adam:
Excellent. Do you see Jesus?

Kristen:
I can see him from behind. He's sitting on the rock. *(Silence)*

Kristen:
The rock we've met on before. He has dreadlocks, long ones. And he helped me up onto the rock. And now I'm me. Adult me. He said it was good to see me again. *(Silence)*

Kristen:
He asked me why I came back. Because I want to remember what we talked about.

Adam:
Do you want to ask him, Kristen, about the conversation you had with him during your first NDE?

Kristen:
We're already having the conversation.

Adam:
Okay.

Kristen:
I'm just having trouble hearing him.

Kristen:
He said I had to go back because Lily needed me.

Kristen:
And Harland needed me.

Kristen:
And he reminded me that when I went back into my body, Laddie was licking my face.

Adam:
And who was that? Was that your dog?

Kristen:
That was the dog.

Adam:
Is that the collie?

Kristen:
Yeah. *(Silence)*

Kristen:
Hey, hold on. (Silence)

Kristen:
I asked him why I had to go back and he said, "Because I hadn't done what I came to the planet to do. I wasn't done yet." And I said, "I'm tired of that explanation. I want more detail." And he said that I had contracted with my children to bring them into the world and I had to come back to do that.

> Note: There are some who believe that before we incarnate, we make a life plan. In that life plan, we pick our parents, friends, and our purpose for the upcoming incarnation. In this example, Kristen shares that it was part of her life plan to bring her children into the world and raise them.

Kristen:
And we made a contract that day, that when it was time, he would speak through me to people. That I came back to share his messages.

Adam:
Kristen, what messages did he want you to speak?

Kristen:
They're in the recordings. I've channeled Christ several times. I have some recordings.

Adam:
Okay. Good.

Kristen:
And he also said that my spirit, even if my human form didn't want to, my spirit wanted to be here for the great awakening. That the great awakening that's happening now and the part that I play in it.

Kristen:
One of millions of Christ's consciousness. One of millions of carrying Christ consciousness. The Christ never, the consciousness was never a man. It was spoken through the man. Just like it is now through many others.

> Note: There is a belief that Jesus was an enlightened master who reached the highest state of intellectual development and maturity. Similar to Buddha. This level of enlightenment is referred to as "Christ consciousness."

Kristen:
It's good to see my old friend again.

Kristen:
He said it's time to go to the hospital. The hospital where I OD'd.

Adam:
Okay. To go back now?

Kristen:
Yeah.

Adam:
Okay. Do you want to ask him to go with you and take you back?

Kristen:
He's coming with me.

Adam:
Okay.

Kristen:
We're going back to the door, at the top of the stairs.

> Note: These are the stairs that Kristen saw in two of her NDEs.

And he's standing on the side of the stairs with me. And we're watching as my younger self is pounding on the door begging to be let in. And there's that voice, the voice that says, "I'm not finished yet." It is saying something else I didn't remember before. It's saying to me, "You promised."

Adam:
You promised what?

Kristen:
You promised to do those things.

Adam:
Do you know who that voice is on the other, that you're hearing?

Kristen:
No. I asked Christ. He said, "Does it matter?" It's an androgynous, echoey voice.

Adam:
Does it matter to you?

Kristen:
No. The message matters.

Adam:
Okay.

Kristen:
I made promises, I have to follow through on them. I was so scared. I was so scared to go back to the violence and the hatred. I just wanted it to stop. I wanted to be in the light. But I had to go back. I was so angry that I had to go back. I just didn't want any more of it.

Kristen:
Now we're in a different hospital room. At the end of a high-risk pregnancy.

Adam:
Whose birth?

Kristen:
My son being born.

Adam:
Okay.

Kristen:
And the pain was so much. It was so much pain. Too long it lasted, too long. His heart stopped. His heart stopped. And then they rushed me to surgery, and I tried to leave again, because the pain was too much. My body couldn't take any more pain. It was shutting down. But they restarted my heart. Because I was standing outside of my body, and my baby asked me to come back because he needed his mommy. So I came back.

Kristen:
I came back for Morgan. Because I promised him I would. I had the contract with him. I promised him I would.

Kristen:
And now Christ is taking me to the light where I was before the last NDE. It was like walking into a party, but I couldn't see anybody; I could just hear the laughter and the chattering, and the love. It was all bright light. So bright, and I was like, "I'm finally home. I'm finally home."

Adam:
And is that where you are now?

Kristen:
Yeah.

Adam:
Can you see more clearly than you did the last time?

Kristen:
No, just vague figures moving around. It's more about the feeling.

Adam:
Okay.

Kristen:
And just knowing that that's my true home. This overwhelming love and peace.

Adam:
Is there anyone that you'd like Jesus to bring forward for you to see? Guides? Family members who have crossed over?

Kristen:
I don't feel the need.

Adam:
Okay.

Kristen:
I'm just one with everything. Just one with the . . . How does that phrase go? The peace that passes all understanding.

Adam:
Yeah.

Kristen:
Just one with it. I don't have a form. I'm just light.

Adam:
Just embrace it. Just let it move through you.

Kristen:
Oh yeah. I love coming here.

Adam:
Is Jesus still with you?

Kristen:
Yes.

Kristen:
He's saying when I'm done here—and I have the choice to leave anytime I want to—that this light is my home.

Adam:
When you have the choice to leave where? Earth or where you are now?

Kristen:
Leave Earth.

Adam:
Okay.

Kristen:
I fulfilled all my promises, and I'm just here for the awakening, however long that lasts, because I chose to be. On Earth. Completely at peace.

Adam:
Good. You're doing great. Do you have any other questions or anything you want to ask Jesus or the light or—?

Kristen:
No. I'm good.

Adam:
Is there anything in your life, Kristen, that you would like healing for, to ask Jesus or the light for?

Kristen:
Not that I don't already work with every day.

Adam:
Okay. Okay good.

Kristen:
I love coming here. I come here actually pretty often. I'm ready.

Adam:
Okay. Any last words? Anything you want to say to anyone wherever you are right now?

Kristen:
Just thanking Christ for coming with me on this journey. And of course my dog who came with me too.

Adam:
You want to give them a big hug goodbye?

Kristen:
Oh, yeah.

CHAPTER X

AMANDA

Amanda's NDE account is a profound example of someone who leaves their body during a physical death and returns with new mystical abilities. I knew of Amanda's near-death story as well as her reputation as a brilliant healer. Amanda is the only participant in the study that I proactively reached out to about volunteering for this research. What I find most fascinating about Amanda's story is the continued connection she's had with the beings she met during her time out of body.

Amanda's NDE Account

Amanda: Okay. So in 1976, I was a college student. I was driving down the road, just a typical day and what happened next was a total shock. A drunk driver ran me off the road. And the next thing I remember is somebody carrying me into the hospital. I don't even know who it was. I just was being carried in somebody's arms. Big arms. A man's arms. And he brought me into the hospital, and they looked at me in the emergency room and pronounced me dead. They said, "Oh, wow, we've got another DOA." And then they saw me move or something that indicated I wasn't dead and put me in a room.

I was in the room only I think a minute, and I left my body and rose above it to the ceiling. One of the strongest memories was floating on the ceiling. It felt like the ceiling was limiting me for a while. Like I was just sliding along the ceiling and it was hitting my back. I was very conscious of what that felt like. And I was looking at my body below on the hospital gurney and thinking, "Wow! Aren't I supposed to be in that body?" You know, it was like I was observing my body, but I felt very detached from it. So then, right about the time where I said, "Wow! Aren't I supposed to be there instead of here?" they started wheeling me down the hall very fast like, you know to surgery. And the whole time they were reeling me down the gurney, I was sliding along the ceiling keeping above where I was physically below.

And then I remember hearing everything but having a lot of blackouts. And at one point the nurse came up to me, put on a mask to give me anesthesia, and that's when I left the room and I floated up. It felt like I went like backwards right through the ceiling and ended up in this gray room. I call it a gray room. It felt like it was a reception area, as bizarre as that is.

There was one being glowing with light standing there, and she looked at me and said,

"Oh! You're not supposed to be here. It's not your time."

And I was also looking down and noticing I wasn't walking—I was floating. Floating through the air while I was having this conversation with the radiant being, which I later figured out was an angel.

Anyway, and it was a woman angel. I don't know why people sometimes say angels don't have a gender. They definitely look male or female to me. Anyway, I looked off to the right of me, and I noticed there was a huge tunnel of light. Gorgeous beautiful lights coming from it that were like a kaleidoscope. The most bright neon lights you can imagine. And I happened to really like that. You know, I like Christmas lights. I like lighted places and I said, "Oh, I'm going to go there!" And so I got all excited about it. And as I was entering the tunnel, the woman angel was joined by a male angel and she said,

"Oh, you can't go in there. Come back!"

And I said, "No. No. No, I really need to go. I want to explore this."

And, so I was determined to push myself through the tunnel, and what happened next was pretty amazing. It felt like the woman angel just froze me in midair.

She was like, "No! I told you. You can't go." And with all my effort, I was trying to propel myself forward. Yet, I was frozen and couldn't move. And so I was pleading. I was saying,

"Come on! I just really want to see what it's like on the other side. And if you just let me see, you know, that'll be good enough."

And so the two of them kind of whispered between each other and then they went, "Okay. Well, we'll have to escort you because your time is going to be limited and you're really not supposed to—we're really not supposed to let you go there."

So I had the female on my left and the male on my right. And we flew through the tunnel like really fast. But at the same time, there were all these swirling colors, neon bright colors that we were in the middle of. There was like an angelic choir that was humming, and so it was very mesmerizing. Then we got to the other side, and I just stood there. And immediately Jesus appeared. He was definitely Jesus. He had dark brown hair to his shoulders, and he was wearing white, and he had so much light coming out of his eyes. It was like flashlight beams just coming out while he looked at me. And I couldn't see the color of his eyes, but I did notice he was in white, you know with brown hair.

Anyway, he kept looking at me and we communicated telepathically. And he said something about,

"I hope you know how much we love you."

And I was just like speechless—didn't say anything. And he said,

"I hope you know we love you." That's all he was saying and it was telepathic communication. And it felt like a hundred thousand people were just standing around and bathing me in love. It was the most incredible experience of unconditional love that you can't even compare to anything here. I can't explain it. But that's what it felt like. I was in the middle of the stadium, and everybody was cheering and telling me how much they loved me, and I was very surprised by that.

So, then Jesus motioned and made me walk with him. And, of course, we didn't really walk. We were moving our feet, but we were floating through the air, and we sat on a bench in a garden. And the angels that were with me as escorts, I got the feeling they were watching us, but they were staying at a distance.

On the way to the bench, which was in a garden setting, I saw hundreds of angels. I mean beings of light that just were so beautiful. Their wings, by the way, weren't made of feathers. They were made of prisms of light. They look like wings, but they're made out of light, not feathers. And they were all smiling at me, welcoming me. So then Jesus and I sat down, and the other thing that was quite amazing about this garden, that I remember quite vividly, is that the flowers were the most intense color that I can't even describe. Everything was intense. The kaleidoscope and the colors and the tunnel were intense. And then when we got to the garden, the flowers and the trees all glowed. Okay, they all had a glow to them, and he said,

"Well, since you're here only for a short time, I want to show you some things that I think would be beneficial."

And next thing I knew, he said, "Well just look down over there."

And again, he wasn't actually saying the words out loud. He was sending them to me with his mind. And I looked down, and the ground in the garden was glass—see-through. And I looked down, and I could see a city and a lot of lights and, you know, people were real tiny, kind of like if you were, let's say, in the Empire State Building a hundred floors up and you were looking down and everything was really small.

And I was like, "Wow! You know, I've never seen anything like this."

And he said "Well, we're going to look at your life."

And so he gave me a life review. He started showing me movies from the time I was a little girl. I remember just one clip of me being a baby that barely was walking. And then he skipped ahead. He talked about that a little bit, and he said,

"Well, remember how that was. This is what happened with you and this is what you gained out of that challenging situation."

And I was like, "Oh, I never thought of it that way."

And he said, "Well, I want to show you a couple more."

And so he went again back into things that were traumatic in my childhood, and he said, "This was the next thing I want to show you. Remember how that was very difficult?"

And I just nodded, yes, and he said, "Well, this is what you gained from going through that experience." And he did that about five times with me.

I can't remember the particular experiences. It was almost like, when we left the garden, my memory got erased. But something of that stayed with me, and the way I could summarize it is I learned that out of something bad comes something good. That that's what he wanted to impress on me. And he said,

"Don't get too caught up in the human drama of things, because it all leads to something."

And I was like, "Oh. Okay."

And so then, as we were leaving the garden, there's a bunch of angels and they were everywhere. Multitudes of them. And they were cheering. They were really happy. And then the two angels that had escorted me in said,

"Well, it's really time for you to go now. You know, we really didn't even expect you were going to be here this long. But you have to go back and this is the time to do that."

And I protested that. I said, "Oh but it's so wonderful here! I've never felt such love. You all love me and it's really full of bliss and it's beautiful. Why would you send me back to my body that's all crippled and injured?"

And you know, I wasn't very happy. And it was a very hard life. And I do remember saying it just like that, and they said,

"Oh, well, we're still asking you to go back."

And I was like, "No! No, I don't want to do that. I don't know. Don't make me go."

And they said, "Well, we didn't want to have to say this, but your mother is really going to need you, and we're sending you back to help her. And we know you care about her. And also there's a lot you're going to learn about love that you haven't even experienced yet. And you're going to be helping people. And you're going to feel good about that."

And I was like, "Yeah, but I like it here so much better."

And they said, "Well, it's serious because your mother could not survive losing both of you."

And I was like, "What do you mean?"

And they said, "That's all we can tell you. Your mother would not survive losing the both of you. So please go back, take care of your mother. Take care of your family. Help the people you're going to meet. And that's what we're asking you to do. And we know we're asking a lot, but that's what we really would like you to do."

And I was like, "Well, if I have to help my mother, okay," but I said, "I don't want to do it alone. It's already been too hard to take care of everybody by myself."

And just so you know, I was the oldest of eight children and lived in an alcoholic family, and it was really rough. I was expected to take care of everybody including my parents. So, anyway, I said, "Okay. Well, I guess if I'm really needed to help people, I'll go."

And next thing I know, I'm there. They're accelerating my flying, and I go through the tunnel really fast like a blink of an eye. And next thing I know, I slid into my body and it felt like I was sliding into home base at a baseball game.

I experienced the sensation of my feet going into the physical head of my body until I skidded through my whole body and my spiritual feet lined up with my physical feet. That's the best way I can describe it. And the male angel said,

"Oh, good. You're home. You're back now."

He didn't say, "Home." He said, "You're back now."

And, I suddenly sprung up. Sitting up. Like a springboard

maneuvered my back. You know, I'm sitting up from a lying down position. And the doctor in the room, oh my God, his eyes were so wide. He was so surprised. He looked at me and he said,

"You're alive. We thought we lost you. We were getting ready to wheel you to the morgue actually and, wow, you're back! You're here! You're alive! You're well! We saved you."

And I got mad. I got angry with him and said, "You didn't save me. What are you talking about? You had nothing to do with it. They kicked me out. They told me I couldn't stay any longer. They said it wasn't my time. They sent me back. That's the only reason I'm here because I was asked to come back."

And he's like, "You're sounding crazy. You better not say that to anybody or they're not going to let you go home. They'll lock you up in the psychiatric ward."

And I just looked at them. I was fuming. I was angry to be back. I was angry to be with this doctor who was telling me this. And my body was like in a lot of pain because I had a broken neck, injured back, dislocated jaw. You know, I was really a mess from head to toe. And so anyway, he said,

"Well, we'll take care of you. But I suggest you not say anything."

And so then he called in other people and they started tending to me, and he said, "Okay, we're going to admit you, you know—for observation."

And I was like, "Do I have to? I don't really like it here."

And he's like, "Yeah, you have to go into the hospital."

So I was in the hospital and I didn't like it there, and that's what I remember.

Now one of the things also that the doctor had said—I don't want to forget to mention this, as he said,

"Oh, you just imagined all that stuff. Your brain probably wasn't getting enough oxygen. You're hallucinating."

And I got angrier, and said, "I was not hallucinating. I know what I saw."

And he was like, "Oh, you know you better just be quiet and rest."

So I did that. And I was pretty well out of it till the next morning, and then they said, "Well, you know, we did everything we could for you. Now we're going to suggest you just stay in the hospital a couple days and rest."

I absolutely was adamant. I wanted to go home. And they were like,

"With the condition you're in, you want to go home?"

And I said, "Well, back to my apartment."

Anyway, you know, and I talked him into actually releasing me. So basically, I went back to my apartment. I had a roommate from college, and we lived in an old apartment building, and I just went to bed and tried to get some sleep. And I was very groggy, you know, from everything. And I remember feeling like, with all that I was going through, I was probably not going to wake up in the morning. I really expected that I was just going to go home and die that night. But I didn't.

And I was in a lot of pain. I also had a ruptured pelvis. So everything hurt so much. But I woke up the next morning and I was very surprised. I was still alive and I stayed in bed all day. And again, by nighttime, I felt worse because the pain would get worse as the day progressed. And again, I thought,

"Well, I'll just close my eyes. I probably won't make it past tonight either."

And I woke up the next morning, again surprised. I was still here. Well on the third night, the angels came and got me to go back to the other side. They said, "Clearly, you know, there's some things we still need to show you. You're obviously alive and you're determined to be alive. And we're glad you're going to fight to be alive. Maybe it would be easier if we take you on another journey and you could be more, you know, peaceful in the experience."

And I said, "Okay!"

So they took me to the other side again. It was the two angels. And I was shown more things about what happened to people after they passed away. And they took me to different levels. That's kind of what it seemed like. "Oh, over here. Here's a bunch of people. You know, they have a lot to learn. They didn't live a very good life. And here's some people who were much smarter about living."

And then, after being shown a bunch of things, by the end of the night they said,

"Oh, it's almost morning. Time for you to go back in your body."

And they took me back. Of course. I was very exhausted because I'd been up all night. And this continued to happen on and off for two weeks. And then it stopped for a while.

I was in a school by the way. A school on the other side. The next time they took me up, it felt like I was going up somewhere. There were other souls with me. That were in school with me. There were twelve of us in a classroom. And I even remember some of who they were, you know, and it was a very diverse group. Like one was an airline pilot and another was a Mexican farmer. And we were all being shown the same things together. How to help people feel the love of God. Very profound things.

Okay, so then after two weeks of doing that pretty much

every night, I was told that they were going to take a break from showing me things and that I was to rest and just take it easy. Well, I had been in the house the whole time so I made an effort to get out of the house. I thought I'd walk to the corner store. And this was in the middle of a big city. So, as soon as I got outside, and it was dark, these people started running toward me. And this was really happening! This was not my dream or a vision out of body. I had actually managed to go downstairs and go walk down the sidewalk toward the store when a whole bunch of people started coming toward me. About fifteen people surrounded me. And I was feeling very overwhelmed.

And I said, "Why are you talking to me?"

And they said, "Well you have this amazing glow of light. You glow so much that we had to come over and see what was going on with you."

And I was like, "What? What do you mean I glow?"

They said, "You're brighter than any light around. You're just absolutely giving off this light. We've never seen anything like it."

And I was like, "Well, I don't know where that's coming from, but I really don't want—I, I'm tired, and I don't really want everybody following me around."

And they were like, "Well, okay, we'll just leave then."

And they left. So I managed to kind of keep myself intact, if you will, because I was very shy at the time. And there was fifteen people around me. Even if I wasn't injured, it would be very overwhelming, and I just decided to forget the store, and I went back upstairs and went back to bed.

Okay. Well, that's how that went. I took it slow. I tried going to a class one day. I was really badly injured. So it's hard. It was extremely painful to walk. I mean, it felt like I was having labor pains, that's how intense the pain was. Like I was having a baby when I walked. It hurt so much. And I decided, okay—I can't go to school. But I went into the store and I bought a package of light bulbs, because I remembered that we needed light bulbs. And when I picked up a bulb in my hand, it lit up like it would in a lamp. And I was like, "Oh my God, what's going on with that?" You know, and then I walked through the department store and there was a bank of TVs. A wall that had a bunch of TVs on display that were all on to demonstrate the televisions. And when I walked up to them, they all turned off. And when I backed up, all the TVs came back on. I did that three or four times, trying to figure out what in the hell was going on.

And that's when I started noticing that everywhere I walked, the electronics in the store went haywire. Everything! Whatever was on started blinking on and off. The lights were blinking on and off. Employees in the store were saying things like,

"Oh, I think we're having a power outage or something."

No, it was me. You know, so I didn't want to get anybody noticing it was me. So I quickly got out of the store, and that's how things went for the longest time. I would turn electronic things on and off without touching them."

Adam: Awesome. Did you did you ever get an answer about what the angels meant when they said that you had to go back because your mother couldn't go through losing both of you?

Amanda: Yeah, they said mother couldn't survive losing both of us.

Adam: Yeah, did you ever get an answer about that? Did you ever ask your mom about that?

Amanda: No, a few years later. My brother died. He had a sudden accident. He was thirty-four years old. He died instantly.

Yeah, that was the death that they had mentioned. Yeah, and she never really did get over that. He was her favorite. She made it real clear. He was the number one favorite. And the rest of us were kind of like second best. Anyway, um, so to lose him, to her, was like the worst thing that could ever happen.

He was as you say the golden-haired boy; he could do no wrong. You know, he was perfect, to her anyway. And when he died, it was such a shock because he had been selling one of the guns from his gun collection. They pieced together what happened. They asked around town if anyone knew anything. It turned out, the night before he died, he had gone to a bar late at night and asked if somebody wanted to buy one of his guns. Because he had an extensive gun collection, and he wanted to sell one for some reason. So, he was talking to people about selling his gun. And when my mother went there the next morning, because she was going to go visit him at his apartment, she found him dead with a bullet through the heart.

It turned out that the gun went off, and he accidentally shot himself. At least that's the conclusion they came to. The gun was jammed. They figured he was trying to clean it, which you normally would not clean a gun with bullets in it, but he had been drinking.

So I always say the alcohol actually was the cause. Yeah, you know, so anyway, here he was, this young person who died with a bullet through the heart. Yeah, my mother found him, so you can imagine how awful that was.

So anyway, that confirmed that first of all, the near-death experience where I was told, you know, my mother couldn't survive losing both of us was not a hallucination like the doctor said. Yep, wrongfully accused. Let's say, yep. I actually got a prediction.

Finally, I would just add that, and when it is your time or anybody's time, accept it as a reward. It's a wonderful place to go. There's nothing to be afraid of once you pass over into the light. And one of the things I was shown in a later trip is that we actually pick how long we're going to be here—before we are born. So it wasn't an accident that my brother passed away that day. You go whatever way you go. But the day you're going to leave is already decided.

After we wrapped recording Amanda's NDE account, she shared a few questions that she wanted to cover during her regression session.

- What did Jesus tell me in my life review?
- How and why did the angels merge with me?
- Why has it been difficult to meet a new partner?
- What do men see when they look at me?

In our regression session, I took Amanda into a hypnotic state and then set the intention for her to experience whatever serves her soul's greatest good as it related to her NDE. The following is a transcript of Amanda's regression session.

Amanda's NDE Regression

After getting Amanda into a deeply relaxed hypnotic trance, I asked her to use her powerful imagination to visualize a hallway with many doors, with each of the doors representing an experience or a set of memories from her life. I then asked Amanda to find a door that seemed to stand out from the others and walk up to it. Once Amanda arrived at the door, she let me know by saying, "I'm here." Then, I connected Amanda with the intention that we set for the regression and asked her to walk through the door. The below is a verbatim transcription of Amanda's regression session.

Amanda walks through the door—

Adam:
Amanda, tell me your impressions. What do you see?

Amanda:
I see lots of green and blue. I see lights through the . . . Huh, kind of interesting. The fluctuation in temperature. It's cold and then it gets warm.

Amanda:
It's alternating.

Amanda:
Blue, I'm seeing lots of blue. Blue lights, blue everywhere. Feels like energy, but alternates between cold and warm. There's swirling clouds all around me.

Adam:
How does it feel? What are you feeling?

Amanda:
It's interesting because my throat feels very tight. It's hard to swallow.

Adam:
Amanda, are you able to look down and see if you're wearing anything on your feet?

Amanda:
No. Well, I am barefoot. Looks like I have a sock on one foot and nothing on the other.

Adam:
Okay. And can you see what you're wearing?

Amanda:
Nothing unusual. Just jeans and a T-shirt.

Adam:
Okay. And when you look around, do you notice if anyone else is there?

Amanda:
It feels like something may be here. It's here, so weird, cause I'm getting a tight feeling in my neck. (Silence)

Amanda:
I'm getting this tight feeling in my neck. (Silence)

Amanda:
Yeah. So I'm feeling a lot of body pain. My back and my lower pelvic area are in pain. No, it doesn't feel good at all.

Adam:
Okay. So Amanda, you said that you are able to sense people are around you. Can you tell who they are?

Amanda:
No. I'm not seeing anybody.

Adam:
Okay.

Amanda:
It's just an empty space with lots of blue and lots of discomfort.

Adam:
Okay. Amanda, do you see anything within the blue? Are there any other colors? Are there any other, as you're looking around, do you see any kind of landmarks or structures or anything?

Amanda:
Something slender is standing next to me.

Adam:
Okay, good. Who is it?

Amanda:
I don't know. He's not saying.

Adam:
Are you able to ask? Can you ask?

Amanda:
I can sense that they're making sure I'm okay. But I can't see them.

Adam:
Okay. Can you ask them to make themselves known? To appear so you can see them? (Silence) Anything coming, Amanda? Are they manifesting at all?

Amanda:
How is it possible that it feels like Jesus is looking at me to see if I'm okay? He's talking to me and saying, "It's okay. It's okay. Everything is good."

Adam:
So he's telling you everything's okay?

Amanda:
Yes.

Amanda:
Well, he's telling me I'm okay.

Adam:
Good. Can you see Jesus? Or are you just sensing him?

Amanda:
I'm not seeing him. My eyes are really tired. I don't feel like opening them.

Adam:
Okay. Can you ask Jesus where you are?

Amanda:
Part of the reason that my eyes are heavy is that most of my back, it really hurts a lot. And I'm afraid because I know what's going on, and I have such a poor body. (Silence) I'm being heard. He's telling me to just relax, let the pain go. It's all basically from my shoulders down and knees.

Adam:
Can you ask him where the pain is coming from, what's causing it?

Amanda:
Yeah. A car crash.

Adam:
Okay. Okay.

Amanda:
I got slammed around in the car. (Silence)

Adam:
And as you look around, Amanda, are you seeing anything else?

Amanda:
Well, it's interesting because I'm seeing a door, like a big entrance. It's like an iron door with bars on it.

Adam:
So it's an ancient door with bars on it, you're saying?

Amanda:
Yeah. It's like a prison door.

Adam:
Oh, like a prison door. Okay. Can you see what's on the other side?

Amanda:
I can't see that. Hold on. (Silence)

Adam:
Are you able to walk through the door at all?

Amanda:
Yeah, I'm walking through the door and I'm actually seeing a woman chained to a wall.

Adam:
And do you know who the woman is?

Amanda:
No idea. I really wonder if it isn't—(Silence)

Adam:
If it isn't what now?

Amanda:
How can I say this? Something that women should have kind of . . . It's something I saw a long time ago. But I'm remembering seeing the woman chained to the wall.

Adam:
Do you get—

Amanda:
And it's showing up because it's the memory of seeing her. It's showing up because I'm feeling like she looks. Feeling so much discomfort in my body. And she looks like she feels as sad as I do. And so, if I were to let go of the pain, it's kind of like she is the image that comes to mind when I'm focused on the pain. So I think it's all in my imagination of remembering.

Adam:
That's okay. You're being shown it for a reason. I think you've landed at a good place, which you're being shown that as a visual representation of the pain that you're feeling. And as you look around this room, is there anything else there that you're noticing?

Amanda:
Yeah. There's another couple, and they're also chained to the wall next to her. The other women in there are getting the same punishment.

Adam:
Can you ask what happened to them? Or who they are? Can you get any information from them?

Amanda:
Yeah. They told me they're being accused of witchcraft.

Amanda:
And I don't know how I managed to see this, but I'm seeing three women being taken, like they're being accused of being witches.

Adam:
Okay. And can—

Amanda:
And I'm being forced to the door, and I'm afraid what's going to happen to me.

Adam:
Can you ask them how you're related to them or why you're seeing them? What's the connection between you and them?

Amanda:
They're telling me I've been there before. That it's something that I experienced a long time ago. (Silence) And I'm not sure how it is, but while I'm seeing this long-ago remembrance, Jesus is next to me. It seems kind of weird.

Adam:
Yeah.

Amanda:
I'm not sure of why I'm seeing what I went through before.

Adam:
Try not to overanalyze it and just allow it to be. Amanda, why don't you ask Jesus why he's showing this to you or why you're seeing it? (Silence)

Amanda:
He's saying so I can heal. And better understand my predicament. I didn't end up so good.

Adam:
So is Jesus able to help you release that pain? How do you release that pain?

Amanda:
Now he's saying, "Breathe. Breathe and relax."

Adam:
Good.

Amanda: It's a very soothing voice. Like you. He's saying no matter what I think, just breathe and relax and remember it's attached.

Adam:
He said to remember what? It's attached?

Amanda:
It's attached. The past is attached to the now. My back is starting to feel a little better.

Adam:
Good.

Amanda:
My body is starting to remember, and I'm no longer in the prison.

Adam:
You're no longer in the prison, okay. Where are you now?

Amanda·
Now back in the blue mist.

Adam:
And how does it feel to be back in the blue mist now?

Amanda:
Feels very healing, actually. My higher energy is helping the pain to go away. And so now Jesus is saying, "Come over here. Let's go sit over here." I'm sitting on a bench.

Adam:
Is there anything else around the bench, or what does it look like where you're sitting?

Amanda:
Well, it's interesting. The bench is in a garden. Lots of flowers everywhere, beautiful flowers. He's telling me to smell the flowers. You can smell the flowers and let it all go. That I don't have to be in the prison anymore.

Adam:
Do you feel like you've been in prison?

Amanda:
I think I was living life in prison.

Adam:
And so Jesus is freeing you from that?

Amanda:
Yeah. And now he's showing me an interesting image of little kids running around and playing. They're about five years old. I think the little girl is me and my brother is with me. And I'm six and he's like three. We're playing outside. He keeps saying, "Remember the time that you fell and skinned your knee? And it was all scraped up and bleeding?" And he came over and he helped me get up.

Adam:
Your brother helped you get up?

Amanda:
Yes. And now I'm getting a message that my mother's coming over. And she's yelling at me.

Adam:
What's she saying?

Amanda:
And she said, "Clumsy."

Adam:
Oh.

Amanda:
Very clumsy. She says, how come I fell down and skinned my knee? I should do better than that.

Adam:
Is your mother on the other side, Amanda?

Amanda:
No. No. (Silence)

Amanda:
This is Jesus showing me something that started when I was little.

Adam:
Okay.

Amanda:
He's showing me the past again. (Silence)

Amanda:
It's kind of interesting because it's like, as I'm sitting here with him, I'm

getting all these flashes of things that happened. First in the prison. Then I'm in my life with my little brother. And he's comforting me and my mother is not happy with me; she's always mad at me. And he tries to be there for me, and then I feel really bad because my mother's mad at me.

Adam:
You feel bad because your mother's mad at you?

Amanda:
Yeah. Always mad at me. I don't think she likes me.

Adam:
Can you ask Jesus why he's showing you this memory of your mother?

Amanda:
Just telling me that sometimes you can't believe people, that sometimes they just are that way. You don't have to believe them. He's telling me I didn't do anything wrong. I didn't do anything bad, but my mother just likes to be mad.

Adam:
Amanda, are there any beliefs that you have about yourself that come from your mother always being mad at you? (Silence)

Amanda:
No, I don't think it's about me. I just think people get mad too easy.

Adam:
Okay.

Amanda:
But she had a lot of problems, I think. But when I was little, I couldn't understand. Jesus is showing me that I wasn't doing anything wrong. I just fell and skinned my knee. I wanted my mother to comfort me and instead, she gets mad. (Silence) I'm glad my little brother was nicer to me.

Now, I'm getting another scene, and I'm a lot older. Jesus is showing me that I'm nine, or somewhere in there, and I'm upstairs in the house. (Silence) And my mother is yelling at me again. I don't know what it's about this time, but she's always yelling at me. I don't know why she's always unhappy.

Adam:
Can you ask her? Are you able to ask her why she's always mad?

Amanda:
She's always unhappy because life is tough. (Silence) She just says, "I have

no idea why life has been tough for me. Why can't you do a better job?" She only wants me to do it right and I always screw up.

Adam:
Amanda, do you want to tell your mom how she's made you feel by saying those things to you and by communicating that to you?

Amanda:
Well, she makes me feel like she doesn't love me, and she tells me that she doesn't love me. And she's trying to teach me a lesson.

Adam:
What lesson is she trying to teach you? (Silence)

Amanda:
That I'm supposed to be her helper and I'm supposed to do it perfect. Why can't I do it perfect when she always shows me how to do something? And why am I always being a bother?

Adam:
And do you believe those things that she's saying to you?

Amanda:
Yeah, I do.

Adam:
Can you share with your mom how she's made you feel? And how that's impacted your life?

Amanda:
I don't think she's going to hear me. If I say anything, she tells me I'm being selfish.

Adam:
What if you were to tell her that this is your time to speak and she has to listen to you? Why don't you give that a try? And just tell her what she's done to you, tell her how that's made you feel your entire life.

Amanda:
Well, I told her but she is, how can I say this? She can do no wrong. I'm the one with the problem. She thinks I'm the one with the problem.

Adam:
Is Jesus still there with you?

Amanda:
Yeah.

Adam:
Perhaps have Jesus ask your mother why she's so harsh on you?

Amanda:
Well, Jesus is asking her. She says, "I don't . . ." She acts very defensive. She's telling him, "Well, you would think the same thing as me if you were in my shoes. And I've been through a lot in life. I'm doing everything right. I just want my daughter to do everything right. And why can't she be more like I want her to be?"

Adam:
And what is Jesus saying back? How does Jesus respond to that?

Amanda:
Well, Jesus is talking to her. He can't get anything through to her. It's not possible. He's saying to me the best thing is just to forgive your mother. She doesn't know what she's doing. Just be a good girl. Be as nice to her as you can. Don't think anything about what she says too much. She's got problems.

Adam:
So are you able to see now, Amanda, that belief that you had about yourself coming from what your mom said to you over the years is not the truth? Are you able to see that now?

Amanda:
I see that people can be pretty critical. I learned how to do so much, but I never learned how to not hurt my mother. No matter how good I was, it was never enough. I was never enough. Jesus is showing me that my mother is in a lot of pain. A lot of pain. All the bad things that happened to her, she took it out on me. But he's comforting me and telling me I didn't do anything wrong. It's just that my mother has problems, and she thinks it's me that has the problem.

Adam:
And who do you believe, Jesus or your mother?

Amanda:
I think Jesus knows me best.

Adam:
Okay.

Amanda:
He just knows what's in my heart. He just knows I'm a good person. It's my mother who never got to know me.

Adam:

Can you ask Jesus why you chose the mom you did in this life? What lesson you were supposed to learn from her?

> Note: There is a belief that before we incarnate as humans, we plan our future life out. We identify experiences that our soul wishes to have and plan accordingly. We plan scenarios that help us work through our karma. We even pick our parents, children, etc. Many have seen this life planning process in both NDEs and life between lives regressions.

Amanda:

Well, it's kind of interesting because he's saying I chose this assignment to take care of the family, because my mother had too many problems to handle it herself. We had hoped that she had learned from me. I hope that's true, but she didn't really let the love in. So she's desperate for love, and she had me thinking that I'd be the solution. And she kept having more and more babies, all because she wanted to be loved but she never felt it. I volunteered to be there, taking care of my sisters and brothers. Otherwise, they would've suffered too much. I was there to teach my mother how to be a mother and that's what Jesus helped me to understand, that I wasn't going to get what I needed from my mom because I was there on an assignment.

Adam:

So you're able to see then, that none of what happened was your fault then, right? I mean, you can see that.

Amanda:

Right.

Adam:

Now you can see the reasons.

Amanda:

Yeah. I didn't do anything wrong. She just didn't know how to love anybody. And then she loved my brother. She did learn how to love him after me. But I was the first one, and she didn't know how to love me, so she just didn't.

Adam:

And are you able to release those feelings and emotions that you've had related to your mother? Can you let those go right now? Can you give them to Jesus?

Amanda:

I give them to Jesus, but I still think it's pretty sad that being nice to her through all the, let's see, sixty-five years that I was alive and she was here, she never learned. Never learned a thing.

Amanda:
And all those babies that she wanted, all so they could love her. She never really learned about love. I guess she'd have to go to another lifetime to learn that.

Adam:
Can you ask Jesus if it's okay for you to release those feelings of sadness about your mother?

Amanda:
I just think some people just waste their life because they're so sad. They don't learn. They just keep doing the same thing over and over again in life. I mean, not to be sad about that. (Silence)

Adam:
So Amanda, it looks like Jesus is giving you a little bit of a life review right now, or at least showing you some memories from your current life. I know when you had your near-death experience, Jesus gave you a life review then too. And, you couldn't remember what Jesus told you in that life review. Are you able to ask him to clarify or remind you what he said in that experience?

Amanda:
Yeah. Now I am. It's becoming clearer, that it's clear that sometimes you come into a life with challenges and you can grow. Sometimes, we come to teach, and, while I didn't know how smart I was, he told me I was a tremendous teacher.

Adam:
That's really interesting, isn't it? I mean, the fact that you came here to teach but you were made to feel as though you weren't smart enough.

Amanda:
Right.

Amanda:
Yeah. People get things all mixed up. They think if you're young in age, you're dumb and if you're old, you must be smart. Or you're smarter. But that's not really how it works.

Amanda:
It's not how old you are, it's how fast you learn. And so interesting really, but the scene is changing now.

Adam:
Okay.

Amanda:
And Jesus is showing me a time that I was real little, and my father was forcing me roughly into the car. It was the time that he took me to an orphanage and left me there all day. I felt very abandoned because he threatened that if I didn't listen to my mother and do everything she said, that they were never going to see me again, that they were going to leave me there. I was very scared, so scared. I was sick to my stomach. I couldn't believe they would just leave me there. Sometimes, he was a good daddy, and right now, he was just leaving me at the orphanage, threatening never to come back if I didn't do everything my mother said. Jesus is showing me that with all the feelings and all the pain of being three and being abandoned.

Amanda:
I'm thinking I'm never going to see my little brother again. I'm barely loved. And I look afraid all the time because they kept threatening to send me back. Eventually, my father got me. And so Jesus is showing me that. I'm saying, "How come they were so mean to me, that they would do that?" And he said that I was, uh, that both my parents were inexperienced. And my mother always wanted to punish me. And sometimes, rather than argue with her, dad would just do whatever she wanted to do to punish me. He didn't want to punish me at all. But if he didn't punish me, then he wouldn't get what he wanted, so I was a bargaining tool. (Silence)

Amanda:
And so being in the middle of the two of them is really rough. My father could only be nice when my mother wasn't looking. So Jesus told me that to remember that both of them had problems, and that it wasn't fair to me, but life isn't fair.

Amanda:
That life isn't fair, but I did agree to take on the assignment to be the teacher to them.

Adam:
What was the lesson you were supposed to learn from that?

Amanda:
The lesson that I was supposed to learn from that is sometimes what I

want doesn't end up being the first priority. And to be strong and to just keep doing what I felt in my heart was right.

Adam:
That's beautiful.

Amanda:
And that, he says, people don't get treated fairly but to keep going, to know that you're going to be rewarded in the end. And not always in the moment. But good things happen. And to have faith. (Silence)

Adam:
So Amanda, with Jesus still there, I know one of the questions you had about your NDE was how and why the angels merged with you. Did you want to ask Jesus about that to clarify?

Amanda:
Yeah. I would like to ask about that. So, Jesus says because I'm not only a teacher, I'm a messenger. The best way to be a messenger is to have other messengers help me. And so I get to see things other people don't see. (Silence)

Adam:
And how did they merge with you? What was the process?

Amanda:
Dispersing at the cellular level. That one thing can become another, just like . . . It's weird. The one that comes to mind is a shape-shifter. He's saying that cellular changes can happen to anything. Things can merge with other things. Things change shape and form. It's a whole bunch of physical things going on that people don't know about. And so they can merge with me on a cellular level so that basically, in my DNA, my very DNA, there's three things, not just one. Which is kind of unusual but it works.

Adam:
So Jesus is saying that you're three beings in one now?

Amanda:
Yeah.

Adam:
That's awesome.

Amanda:
Yeah, well, it feels like that. It was, when it started happening, I was getting very strange body sensations. They were kind of hard to describe

but, anyway, I could feel like all of my torso changed. My posture changed, all kinds of things. And I had a doctor that was helping me through the changes. The angels just decided that I would be an unusual person. (Silence) Kind of can't explain that. That's what he says.

Adam:
Okay. Do you have any other questions you want to ask him about the angels?

Amanda:
Yeah.

Amanda asks, "So is there anything I'm supposed to know about this, because I don't even understand it (laughing). Kind of out there. What am I supposed to know that I don't know about this already?"

(Laughing) "You'll soon find out." Okay. Keep me in suspense already. It might explain why my ribcage got so changed from the injury. But I'm thinking in my head, "Am I supposed to be three beings in one?" That's just kind of odd. It's hard to comprehend.

Adam:
Yeah. Amanda, I know you had a couple of other questions you wanted to ask. One of those questions was related to your dating life and why it's been so difficult for you to meet a partner. Did you want to ask Jesus that question while you have him here?

Amanda:
Yeah. I would like to ask that. It's a puzzle because I'm good to people, I'm flexible, I'm easygoing. Devoted in my relationships to my friends and my partners. I really don't know what's with all that.

(Silence) The only thing I'm getting as an answer is just learn to feel good every day.

Adam:
Do you want to ask him what that means, why he's giving you that answer?

Amanda:
Well, I'm asking. I'm getting kind of whispers of things. That feeling good every day means that I don't really have to have somebody here, even though I'd like to have company. But it doesn't have to be a necessity. I'm learning just to live in peace.

Adam:
Is it in your plan to meet somebody? Can you ask him that question?

Amanda:
I can. I'll ask. (Silence) The answer I'm getting is that I will meet who I meet. And for the time being, I'm just going to have to be prepared for people coming and going. Not staying for long. It's just a lot going on.

Adam:
Amanda, another related question you have, what do men see when they look at you?

Amanda:
Yeah. Well, they like me. They like what they see. They like my energy. They like me. It's like energy. I'm in a place that feels really good, and they don't feel so good about themselves and they leave. It's like them not feeling good about themselves is not compatible with me feeling good about myself. I'm being shown that's a real struggle with them.

Amanda:
Yeah. People struggle. All people. But especially men right now. They are struggling about feeling good about themselves. And so when I'm good with everything, they feel like we're not a match.

Adam:
Ah, because your energy is in a more positive—. Is he saying because your energy is in a more positive place than theirs, that's why you're not matching?

Amanda:
Yeah, because they're unhappy. And then that basically, I can't make them happy. They have to find that happiness inside. (Silence)

Adam:
Amanda, is there anything else that Jesus wants to show you while you're home?

Amanda:
No, let me ask. (Silence) I don't think, he's just telling me to forgive everyone who didn't understand. Everyone who could've been better to me, kinder and more accepting, to just forgive them. They have no idea and they're struggling. I know I struggle too, but he's saying I have way more of an idea than most people. And until people feel good about themselves, I can't be around them too long. I know it's kind of weird because I'm nice to people and I compliment them and such. But people don't feel like they can be happy. They can't be around me. It would take a happy person to be around me. Jesus is showing me that until I meet

someone who's actually happy, then it's going to be my solo journey.
(Silence)

Amanda:
I do tend to attract the gloomy people. But until a person's really happy with themselves, I don't feel like spending a lot of time with them.

Adam:
Yeah.

Amanda:
There's a lot of unhappy people in the world right now. So I don't know. I don't know where to be right now, because I can be nice to people and I like being nice to people.

And somebody is coming over. I feel like I'm returning back from the other side right now.

Adam:
What's happening, Amanda?

Amanda:
I'm coming out of the other side journey

Adam:
Oh, okay. Where are you now?

Amanda:
Back at my house seeing people come over. They look for things to criticize. It could be, oh, why are you putting that picture up? Or I don't like the colors you picked, or oh, you should get a new floor. Looks like you have three cats. It's an unending critical stream of people I've invited over. It's amazing how that pours out of them. I've just come to the realization that they're critical because they don't understand how I got here. So they want to diminish my place. They're trying to feel better about themselves, so they do that by criticizing me or my place.

Adam:
Do you want to ask Jesus why you keep attracting these people into your life?

Amanda:
Yeah, good question. I'll tell you, I've never had people be so critical of my house and things. It's crazy. They always find something. It's like they look with a magnifying glass really good. I could clean the house for ten days and it doesn't matter. They come over and pick it apart. It's gotten

to the point, it's like maybe stop inviting people. It's a puzzle. Why would someone do that? But now I understand. Now I understand.

Adam:
And what's the reason why?

Amanda:
That they don't feel good about themselves.

Adam:
Yeah.

Amanda:
Yeah.

Adam:
But how come they're attracted to you? How come they keep getting welcomed into your life?

Amanda:
Because I'm one of the kindest people you'll ever meet. And when I'm kind to somebody, they don't know how to accept that. People are not having the experience in being treated well, or feeling like they are. So they come to me, knowing that I will treat them well. But then they don't treat me well. I'm not sure how to change that, how to get someone who is on the same page. Someone who doesn't have to be critical to feel better about themselves. It's almost like there's an energy in friends, maybe from earlier years or something. But now I know that's them. I don't need to keep changing colors or take the picture down just because they don't like it. (Silence)

Amanda:
And they're not unusual pictures. That's the funny part. I have pictures of nature. A couple pictures of angels. Mostly, ocean pictures.

Adam:
Okay.

Amanda:
The only other thing that is coming through, which is kind of interesting, is two things. I wouldn't say it's a full answer, but it's kind of maybe something to think about. The first thing was tolerance for people that are not in as good of a place as myself. Just be tolerant and know that they haven't made the choice to be there yet. Some of them don't understand what it's like to be in a place and feeling good. The other thing I'm being told is the timing is just not there yet. But boy, I sure have

to be patient on that one. Ten years is a long time to hope somebody shows up. *(Silence)*

Adam:
All right. Let's get ready to come out of the hypnotic state.

Amanda:
I will say, some intense stuff came through during the regression.

Adam:
Yeah. Well—

Amanda:
I wasn't even verbalizing it, but I can tell you my back, oh my gosh. I learned to be tolerant of pain because of past injuries. But wow, it was like the car crash injuries with your helping me get to that space was like my body was reliving it.

Adam:
Are you still feeling any pain?

Amanda:
No, it's gone now.

Adam:
Okay. Good. Okay.

Amanda:
Yeah. It was interesting, though. It was like, holy cow, is this what my back used to feel like? I'm glad it doesn't feel like that anymore.

Adam:
Yeah.

Amanda:
And then the other thing is just a profound releasing of tears, which I don't do very often. Again, it's knowing that life is such a miracle and people waste so much time. It's just how it is. But I'm going to feel more at ease. Also, now that I've let go of that sadness about how people just don't want things really bad. So I call them slow learners. I'm not saying I'm a fast learner myself, but I'm faster than some. That's becoming pretty obvious.

CHAPTER XI

WHAT HAPPENS TO US WHEN WE DIE

Explaining the Differences in Near-Death Experiences

As you've read through the various NDE accounts and subsequent regressions in this book, you probably observed that there were differences, albeit some slight, in each participant's experience. For example, at least half of the volunteers met Jesus in both their NDEs and regression. However, not all of the participants had the same experience with Jesus. One of the participants experienced Jesus as Lord and Savior, very similar to how Jesus is portrayed in the New Testament. Others experienced Jesus as more of an "Ascended Master" and Spirit Guide. Other participants experienced more interaction and engagement with angels than with Jesus. And others experienced connections with aliens, cosmic beings, and phenomena not tied to any religious belief.

The aforementioned begs the question, "Why do people experience differences in their NDEs, while out of body?" The simple answer is, I can't say for sure. Nobody can. However, there is a theory that I subscribe to that I think makes a lot of sense. In the book *Seth Speaks—The Eternal Validity of the Soul*, published in 1972, its author, Jane Roberts, channels a discarnate entity named Seth. Seth, who no longer incarnates in the physical form, describes himself as a "teacher." Seth tells Roberts that he has come through to have his words recorded and later published as a book to help people understand the nature of self and reality. Within the material, Seth speaks about what happens to us when we die.

> "A belief in hell fires can cause you to hallucinate Hades' conditions. A belief in a stereotyped heaven can result in a hallucination of heavenly conditions. You always form your own reality according to your ideas and expectations. This is the nature of consciousness in whatever reality it finds itself. Such hallucinations, I assure you, are temporary. [...] There are teachers to explain the conditions and circumstances. You are not left alone, therefore, lost in mazes of hallucination. You may or may not realize immediately that you are dead in physical terms. First of all, it should be obvious from what I have said so far that there is no one after-death reality, but [that] each experience is different. Generally speaking, however, there are dimensions into which these individual experiences will fall. For example, there is an initial stage for those who are still focused strongly in physical reality, and for those who need a period of recuperation and rest. On this level there will be hospitals and rest homes. The patients do not yet realize that there is nothing wrong with them at all. [...] It goes without saying

that the hospitals and training centers are not physical in your terms. They are often, in fact, maintained en masse by the guides who carry out the necessary plans. Now you may call this mass hallucination if you will. The fact is that to those encountering that reality, the events are quite real."

– Roberts, 1972

In other words, Seth is saying that when we die, we tend to see what we expect to see. And whether or not you believe that Jane Roberts was channeling messages from Seth, the logic is sound. What we know from evidence gathered in NDEs and out-of-body experience research is that when a soul pops out of its body, it doesn't forget the human/physical life it leaves behind. As I wrote about in the Hypnotic Regression and NDEs chapter, we have local and nonlocal memory. I believe that nonlocal memory is what allows us to recall our past lives and between lives under hypnosis. And when we leave our bodies, our most recent life is what's top of mind for us. So, if we believe wholeheartedly that we'll see Jesus in heaven when we die, there's a good chance that we'd freak out if we saw something different. In other words, when we do die and cross over, we may well see what we'd expect to. And then, as we go through the healing process and acclimate to our new dimensional environment, more and more truths get exposed that allow us to shed old belief patterns formed in this life.

Another theory, which is slightly different than Seth's, is that we create our reality in the afterlife. In other words, we can live out whatever experiences we wish to have once we leave our body.

Neither theory, nor any other "What happens to us when we die?" theory, is scientifically provable. All we have is anecdotal evidence from what people have experienced through their own NDEs/OBEs, psychic communication, plant medicines, and deep meditation.

However, most NDE research (including the regressions in this book) does show that regardless of how different our afterlife experiences are from each other, there are important similarities that most people note.

Looking at Death Metaphorically

THE STREAM AND THE WHIRLPOOL

"Just, for example, as a whirlpool in water, you could say because you have a skin you have a definite shape you have a definite form. All right? Here is a flow of water, and suddenly it does a whirlpool, and it goes on. The whirlpool is a definite form, but no water stays put in it. The whirlpool is something the stream is doing, and exactly the same way, the whole universe is doing each one of us, and I see each one of you today and I recognize you tomorrow, just as I would recognize a whirlpool in a stream. I'd say 'Oh yes, I've seen that whirlpool before, it's just near so-and-so's house on the edge of the stream, and it's always there.' So in the same way when I meet you tomorrow, I recognize you, you're the same whirlpool you were yesterday. But you're moving. The whole world is moving through you, all the cosmic rays, all the food you're eating, the stream of steaks and milk and eggs and everything is just flowing right through you. When you're wiggling the same way, the world is wiggling, the stream is wiggling you." (Watts, 2019)

I love Alan Watts's analogy of the stream and the whirlpool. To me, the stream represents the consciousness of the universe, and the whirlpool is a distinct manifestation of the stream. You can think of each person, animal, plant, rock, etc. as whirlpools in the constant stream of the universe. Of course, as humans, we don't see each other as the stream. Our ego/shadow thrives on individuality, so we see ourselves as the whirlpool. In fact, from the moment we're born, we're conditioned to believe that we are the whirlpool.

"Hi, I am Adam and I'm a certified hypnotherapist, author, dog lover, Reiki Master, yada, yada." Well, that's me defined as a whirlpool. That's me defined by my individuality. Now, if I were to look at myself more metaphysically, I would simply define myself as, "I am." And when I looked out into the stream, I would recognize that I'm not the whirlpool, rather I'm the manifestation of two opposing currents in the stream manifesting itself as a whirlpool. In other words, I'm the universe manifesting itself as Adam Dince. In other words, Adam Dince is not Adam Dince. Adam Dince is "I Am." And I would recognize that everyone else is also consciousness manifesting itself as "I Am" as well. Meaning, we are all part of the flow of consciousness. And outside of the earth plane, at our highest level of consciousness, we're all one.

So, what happens when we die? What happens to a whirlpool after it ceases to function like a whirlpool? The whirlpool goes back to being the stream. And we lose our human form and transition back into pure consciousness.

This is a concept very difficult to grasp intellectually. However, many NDEers and those who have experienced reaching the same mystical realms through other means understand this wholeheartedly.

Similarities in Near-Death Experiences

In the research conducted for this book, everyone who was regressed to the beyond experienced the purest of love. A love that transcends human words or the ability to express. I haven't had the opportunity to experience the type of near-death experience love that research participants felt when they went "home." I have, however, experienced a supernatural type of love. A love that surpasses all understanding. It was during a sacred medicine ceremony facilitated by Shaman Madhu Anand. I experienced the many layers of conditioning, trauma, ego, and whatever else was there melt away. And I was left for a few moments as my purest essence—my soul. And in those moments, I felt the most powerful love for myself and for every other being poured into me and through me. I recall closing my eyes and asking God to never let me forget that feeling and to allow me to stay in this cloud of love forever. Of course, while I still have love in my heart, eventually the supernatural love I experienced in the sacred medicine ceremony wore off. When I've shared my sacred medicine story with people who have had NDEs, they totally understand. Imagine the brightness of the sun. How it only takes a second or two of looking at the sun before it becomes too bright to look at with your bare eyes. That's how powerful and brilliant the love in our hearts is. It's just that we've all been through so much in this human life (and past lives) that it's difficult for us to connect with it. But it's that love that ties us all together in both the present life and afterlife and with All That Is.

Another commonality among NDE/regression accounts is that participants were able to receive important answers and closure regarding current and past-life situations. Answers to questions and closure on things that had remained open for years. In some cases, participants were not given the answers to the questions they had. And in those cases, participants did hear messages or themes like, "It will be revealed in time." or "You already have the answers."

One of my favorite similarities among the NDE/regression experiences is that each of the participants referred to the place they traveled to out of body as "home." Regardless of the differences among accounts, the feeling of being "home" was persistent. The familiarity with the environments and dimensions they went back to was poignant.

Another similarity across NDEs and subsequent regressions was the feeling of disconnection from the physical body. Again, I personally haven't had a near-death experience, but I have had an out-of-body experience, which I described in Chapter II. In my OBE, I felt that freedom of being completely disconnected from my body. It was almost as if I was staring down at a stranger lying in my bed. And I didn't want to return to my body. All I wanted to do once floating freely was to travel elsewhere. I felt so light and magical.

When I first began studying spiritual, mystical experiences, the entire concept of out-of-body experiences seemed so hard to believe. But, once you experience an OBE, you know. There's no more need to believe or read others' accounts. You know they're real. And it's a beautiful gift from the universe that allows us to see how mystical we truly are.

In Conclusion

I wouldn't be telling the truth if I said that my fear of death is completely gone. However, what I have learned throughout my journey is that we are incredibly vast beings. We are so much more than we imagine ourselves to be. In the previous chapters, we examined seven beautiful souls who have had brilliant encounters with the beyond. It is my hope that their NDE stories support you in your journey and that the regression transcripts demonstrate just how thin the veil is. The veil between worlds. The veil between here and there.

Finally, I would like to thank you with all of my heart for taking the time to read this book. It's been a labor of love for me and the volunteers who participated in the research. If there's ever any way I can support you in your journey, please do not hesitate to reach out. Please feel free to visit adamdince.com to contact me.

WORK WITH ADAM

Adam Dince is a certified hypnotherapist through the Institute of Neuro-Linguistic Programming (iNLP) Center and the International Hypnosis Federation (IHF). Adam specializes in regressing clients back to past lives, life between lives regression (LBL), and revisiting current life memories with the goals of healing traumas, removing limiting beliefs, and overcoming other challenging life experiences. Adam believes that hypnotherapy and alternative healing practices are essential components of a strong mind-body-soul connection.

In addition to practicing hypnotherapy, Adam is also a Reiki Master Teacher, sacred medicine facilitator, author, and adjunct professor and is the founder of and healer at Sacred Stairways Hypnotherapy & Healing, located in beautiful Stillwater, Minnesota. If you'd like to work with Adam, here are a few ways to connect:

Book Adam to Speak: Email adam@sacredstairways.com

Schedule a Hypnotherapy Intake Session:
Visit https://sacredstairways.com/book-a-session/

Sign up for Adam's newsletter at
https://backtothebeyond.com/subscribe and receive:

- A complimentary thirty- to forty-minute-long hypnosis audio track that supports relaxation and stress reduction.
- Instructional videos to help you connect with loved ones on the other side.
- Special deals and discounts on products and services.

BIBLIOGRAPHY

Alexander, Dr. Eben (n.d.). *My Experience in Coma (NDE)*. Retrieved from EbenAlexander.com: http://ebenalexander.com/about/my-experience-in-coma/

Dass, R. (n.d.). *Dying Is Absolutely Safe—Awareness Beyond Death*. Retrieved from Ramdass.org: https://www.ramdass.org/dying-is-absolutely-safe/

Hagerty, B. B. (2009, May 22). *Decoding The Mystery Of Near-Death Experiences*. Retrieved from NPR: https://www.npr.org/templates/story/story.php?storyId=104397005

Holden, J., & James, D. (2009). *The Handbook of Near-Death Experiences: Thirty Years of Investigation*. Santa Barbara, CA: Praeger/ABC-CLIO.

Near-Death Experiences (NDEs). (n.d.). Retrieved from University of Virginia Medical School: https://med.virginia.edu/perceptual-studies/our-research/near-death-experiences-ndes/

Ring, K., & Cooper, S. (1997). "Near-Death and Out-of-Body Experiences in the Blind: A Study of Apparent Eyeless Vision." *Journal of Near-Death Studies*, 16, 101–47.

Rivas, T., & Dirven, A. (2010). *Van en naar het Licht [From and to the Light]*. Leeuwarden, The Netherlands: Elikser.

Roberts, J. (1972). *Seth Speaks: The Eternal Validity of the Soul*. San Francisco: New World Library.

Smit, R. H. (2008). "Corroboration of the Dentures Anecdote Involving Veridical Perception in a Near-Death Experience." *Journal of Near-Death Studies*, 27, 47–61.